# the **HIGHLY SENSITIVE**
# **PERSON'S** TOOLKIT

# the **HIGHLY SENSITIVE PERSON'S** TOOLKIT

Everyday Strategies
for Thriving in an
Overstimulating World

ALLISON LEFKOWITZ, LMFT

**ROCKRIDGE
PRESS**

Interior and Cover Designer: Heather Krakora
Art Producer: Meg Baggott
Editor: Vanessa Ta
Production Manager: Giraud Lorber
Production Editor: Melissa Edeburn

ISBN: Print 978-1-64739-076-1 | eBook 978-1-64739-077-8
R0

*I dedicate this book to my family, especially my husband, Damien, and extraordinary dog, Willis, who provided me with unlimited cups of tea, unconditional emotional support, and belly rubs.*

# CONTENTS

# INTRODUCTION

"You feel so much, but you keep going."

At the end of my eight-year participation in an eight-year group practice, I sat quietly, my eyes full of tears and heart full of gratitude as my fellow therapists expressed their wishes for me as I expanded my private practice to a full-time endeavor. The practice, a healing oasis nestled above the busy streets of Madison Avenue in Midtown Manhattan, New York City, had a lovely ritual of giving departing members verbal and written messages of love and support as they moved on to the next phase of their lives.

Though I had known for quite a while I needed to expand my existing private practice, I was absolutely terrified to go out on my own. With the love and support of my irreplaceable mentor, Mary, and, in hindsight, the gift of hotel construction next to my office, I finally decided to leave my nest. The unrelenting jackhammers were the universe's way of letting me know it was time.

As we moved through the goodbye ritual and reflections, one of my colleagues said, "You feel so much, but you just keep going." I noticed my body flinch and tense, my face tighten, and a feeling of anger rise in my chest. I feel SO MUCH and keep going? Though I do believe this fellow therapist's comment was meant as a compliment, it left me feeling a wee bit defensive and also confused. Was there something wrong with how much I feel and experience? Was it a surprise that I could "feel so much" and still function? Was I supposed to collapse if I expressed sadness, anger, or anxiety?

What did my immediate feeling of anger mean? Why was I so conditioned to defend myself when someone brought up my sensitivity?

I had identified as a highly sensitive person (HSP) for several years and had even been given an opportunity to do training about highly sensitive people at my practice. I wondered if that training conveyed the true nature of the highly sensitive person. After I sat with my momentary irritation and anger, I realized how sensitivity can be so misunderstood and how it was part of my mission and calling as a therapist to assist other highly sensitive people to identify their strengths, work through their personal traumas and challenges, and let their positive traits shine. My colleague was right; I can feel so much, and I can keep going. You, my dear highly sensitive human, can, too.

The training I provided did not convey the full strength and power of highly sensitive people and all the gifts we can bring to this world. I know my strength now more than ever because as I write this the world is currently moving through the COVID-19 pandemic.

I am feeling so much, and I am still going. I am holding my own fear, sadness, and grief *and* holding space for my loved ones and my dear clients. I felt the anxiety in the air before the crisis began to crystallize; I felt the rush of panic as I had to leave my office and establish my practice online. I felt the sadness in my neighbors' eyes as we crossed paths on the way to wherever we would take refuge for an undetermined amount of time.

I imagine you relating to these emotions as you read these words. We feel it all.

And. We. Keep. Going.

The goal of this book, as with my clinical work, is not only to provide education, strategies, and resources, but to very simply teach you, empower you, and invite you, to be . . . yourself. All of you. You don't need to be molded, cured, or fixed. I can assure you there is nothing wrong with you. In fact, everything, and I truly mean everything, you need to live your authentic life is within you. You are so very welcome here.

# HOW TO USE THIS BOOK

As highly sensitive people, we find that our physical environments can affect how we receive information. Before you dive into this book, settle into your space and make sure your senses are ready to receive helpful information.

Perhaps you are sitting in your favorite soft chair in your home, a fuzzy blanket draped over your lap, and a furry companion somewhere nearby. Do you need to turn on a light or close the blinds? Do you need to open a window or turn on a fan? Are you cozy? Great, let's keep going.

This book is full of strategies to help you thrive as a highly sensitive person. You can read this book's contents in whatever order you wish, though I do have some recommendations.

This book is written for those who have already identified as highly sensitive. If you are unsure whether you are a highly sensitive person, I recommend taking the HSP self-test found on the website HSPerson.com or in the books of Elaine Aron. If you have only recently discovered that you are a highly sensitive person, read chapter 1, which presents important HSP research.

If you are troubled by particular life circumstances, such as work, self-care, or family relationships, feel free to skip ahead to the chapters that present strategies for addressing those circumstances. If you are aware that you have a trauma history, take the quiz on pages 12–14, and share the results with your therapist—if you are, as I hope, in therapy. Many highly sensitive people do have a trauma history. The quiz will help you distinguish your trauma symptoms from your traits as a highly sensitive person to help you live your authentic life.

I highly recommend that you practice the sensitive core skills outlined at the end of chapter 1 (see page 14) before attempting to implement any of the strategies provided throughout this book. In my clinical practice, I have found these skills enable highly sensitive people to thrive.

In this book, I share, with permission, the stories and experiences of some of my clients. Their names have been changed to protect their privacy.

Be compassionate with yourself as you practice this book's strategies. Creating the life you want takes time and patience. Be kind to yourself as you undertake this journey.

# CHAPTER ONE

# The Highly Sensitive Person

Understanding and defining our highly sensitive selves can be a challenge, especially with the wealth of information and, unfortunately, disinformation that exists. In this chapter, we will take an in-depth look at what it means to be a highly sensitive person as well as discover some of the differences among highly sensitive people. We will discuss what it's like to be a highly sensitive person and how our childhoods and life experiences can color our perceptions of ourselves and our world. Finally, we will discuss how childhood trauma can play a role in the development of highly sensitive people and how symptoms of that trauma can overlap with, or even mimic, some of our traits as highly sensitive people.

# WHAT DOES IT MEAN TO BE A HIGHLY SENSITIVE PERSON?

Research has found that 15 to 20 percent of human beings are highly sensitive (Aron 2010). Because of our finely tuned nervous systems and uniquely organized brains, we highly sensitive people live, breathe, love, work, and connect with the world differently than the majority of the population. We notice subtle changes in the environment and can react strongly to lights, sounds, smells, tastes, and other stimuli. We instinctually live with our ears open, our eyes wide, and our hearts ready to receive.

Beyond sensitivity to our physical environment, highly sensitive people also have an innate ability to be deeply empathic. Some of us define ourselves as empaths. We are walking, talking emotional sponges. Some of us experience our own emotions at a higher level as well. We laugh louder, cry harder, grieve more deeply. Highly sensitive people commonly feel misunderstood or judged by those not highly sensitive. We are told our emotions are "too strong." In cultures where displaying vulnerability or expressing emotions is not the norm, these judgements can be especially prevalent.

We also tend to have complex inner lives and think deeply about ourselves and the world. We can be moved by situations we read about or witness, whether a sad story on the news, a heartbreaking movie, or a grief-filled post on social media. Many of us find the world to be lacking in compassion, empathy, and understanding.

As highly sensitive people, we have an aversion to seeing human suffering utilized for entertainment value (Aron 2010). You will not find many highly sensitive people lining up for the next bloody horror movie or binge-watching the newest zombie TV show. Explaining to friends or family why we haven't watched *Game of Thrones* can be a bit challenging.

High sensitivity is innate, passed down by generations of sensitive ancestors, and is equally distributed across both genders (Aron 2010). This sensitivity is not a result of experiences or intergenerational trauma and is also certainly not a disorder or something to be fixed or cured.

Because some trauma symptoms can mimic HSP traits (such as feeling overwhelmed and overstimulated physically), the highly sensitive person must learn to distinguish between expressions of inborn sensitivity and their past trauma. Through my clinical work with highly sensitive people,

I have found that once they were able to heal past traumas and soothe, calm, and regulate the nervous system, what once was overwhelming or overstimulating was now far more manageable. Through this process of discovering and reorganizing the nervous system, the highly sensitive person has better access to their strengths and sensitive superpowers. Later in this chapter, I will provide a list of questions to help you begin to sort traits of your highly sensitive nature from your trauma symptoms.

Studies of highly sensitive nervous systems of more than 100 animals species—including primates, birds, and fruit flies—show that these animals responded to their environment by first pausing and reflecting on a stimulus, then reacting. These sensitive animals prefer to "do it once and do it right" (Wolf et al. 2008). Their more highly attuned senses also make them better able to keep safe from predators, find food, and seek a mate. Because of their highly sensitive systems, they have a better chance of survival.

Highly sensitive people also possess vantage sensitivity, a propensity to benefit disproportionately from a positive environment or experience when compared with those not as sensitive. Given the right environment, a highly sensitive child is likely to excel academically and socially and develop their fullest potential.

Unfortunately, highly sensitive people are also more likely to be impacted negatively by an adverse environment or experience when compared with those not as sensitive. This negative impact is especially true when rooted in childhood experiences or with trauma of various forms throughout one's life (de Villiers et al. 2018).

Highly sensitive people are also described as having sensory processing sensitivity defined by four primary indicators as summarized by the acronym DOES (Aron 2010):

**D:** Depth of Processing—take in high degree of sensory information and subtleties from the environment

**O:** Overstimulation—become physically or emotionally overwhelmed by one's environment

**E:** Emotional Responsiveness or Empathy—have strong emotional responses to stimuli or the ability to feel the emotions of others

**S:** Subtle Stimuli Awareness—able to pick up on nuances in self and environments

## Depth of Processing

The HSP brain is uniquely wired. Brain scans reveal higher activity in the insula, which controls enhanced perception and awareness, than in non-HSP brains (Acevedo et al. 2014). HSP brains are also wired to pause and reflect before engaging. We prefer, just like the sensitive animal species of the previously mentioned studies, to stop and take in all relevant information before we act. In the modern world, it could look like researching and reading the reviews before buying something. Who wants to trek back to the post office? Not highly sensitive people!

## Overstimulation

Because our highly sensitive nervous systems are taking in more sensory information, highly sensitive people are prone to overstimulation. In my experience as both a highly sensitive person and someone who works with them, I find that the elements of overstimulation usually fall into three categories.

SOCIAL: Examples include large crowds, loud parties, and other social situations. There might be a need or desire to hide, rest, or nap after social stimulation.

PHYSICAL/ENVIRONMENTAL: Examples include lights, itchy fabrics, strong smells, and loud noises. A highly sensitive person may feel easily overwhelmed especially with shifts, changes, or large environmental events. We can be more greatly affected emotionally and physically by shifts in the moon and planetary systems or changes in barometric pressure and humidity.

EMOTIONAL: An example includes being a part of, or even just witnessing, a bad argument.

## Emotional Responsiveness/Empathy

The highly sensitive person's emotional responsiveness and deep empathy is, at least in my opinion, one of the greatest hallmarks of the trait and one of the greatest gifts to bring to personal and professional relationships. We have the ability to understand intellectually another's situation so much so that we can literally feel the same emotions and physical sensations as another person. This responsiveness is also detectable in scans of HSP brains that show more active mirror neurons, which control empathy and emotion, than those of people less sensitive.

## Subtle Stimuli Awareness

Highly sensitive people are natural detectives, often noticing subtle details that less sensitive individuals may miss, such as nonverbal cues and small changes in the environment. Their keen sensory awareness often means knowing how and when to make small adjustments and is one of the many reasons highly sensitive people are wonderful healers, artists, designers, writers, and musicians. They intuitively know how to hit the right notes, slightly change a color palette, or gently reframe a conversation (Aron 2020).

# DEEPENING AWARENESS OF OUR HIGHLY SENSITIVE SELVES:
## On Introverts, Extroverts, and Empaths

Introverts as a rule don't need people for joy or energy and love alone time. Often preferring solo activities, the introvert does like to socialize occasionally. An extrovert gets energy and joy from meeting and connecting with new people. An empath can be introverted or extroverted and is someone who feels the emotions of another. In her book *The Highly Sensitive Person*, Elaine Aron estimates that 70 percent of highly sensitive people are also introverts (but not all introverts are highly sensitive people or empaths). Many people believe that highly sensitive people cannot be extroverted when, in fact, an estimated 30 percent are! In contrast, a good number of empaths are also likely to be highly sensitive people.

The literature on these classifications can be confusing and contradictory, however. Jacquelyn Strickland, licensed professional counselor, coach, and HSP researcher, attempted to bring clarity to these issues, especially surrounding introversion and extroversion in relation to the highly sensitive person (Strickland 2018). One of the main sources she examined is the popular book by Susan Cain, *Quiet: The Power of Introverts in a World That Can't Stop Talking*. While Strickland agreed with Cain's definition of the highly sensitive introvert as being "a [person] of contemplation," she took issue with Cain's assertion that the highly sensitive extrovert is "a [person] of action," pointing out that the highly sensitive extrovert actually desires a combination of both action and quiet contemplation.

For a discussion of the relationships between the highly sensitive person and the empath, Dr. Judith Orloff's book *The Empath's Survival Guide: Life Strategies for Sensitive People* is a great resource. She finds that while both the highly sensitive person who does and does not identify as an empath is well attuned to those around them, the empath actually mirrors the experiences of others, which is not the case with those who are not empaths. Empaths also tend to have a stronger link between their emotional and physical bodies and, when overwhelmed with intense emotions, can develop autoimmune disorders, chronic fatigue, and depression and anxiety disorders.

Though labels can serve to define and normalize, they can also be limiting. Some may think of all those labeled as highly sensitive as being the same, when in actuality they, like anyone human, have a unique mix of traits.

Having a clear definition and attuned sense of who we are is important, but I believe the most helpful viewpoint for highly sensitive people is not to be so fixated on clearly defining oneself but on developing awareness of our unique combination of traits and looking for ways to honor and tend to our highly sensitive selves, whether introverted, extroverted, empathetic, or a gorgeous cornucopia of them all!

# SENSITIVES IN THE WILD: EXISTING IN A LESS THAN SENSITIVE WORLD

One rainy day last spring, my client, Carl, arrived 10 minutes late to our weekly psychotherapy session. He was a new client, only about three or four sessions in, and had sought therapy because he thought he might be "too emotional" or "too much," as family members, bosses, and ex-partners had reflected to him. He burst into the office, clearly overstimulated, his face streaked with tears. He immediately lay down on the couch (I'm not a Freudian psychologist, so this isn't a usual occurrence) and began to weep.

"This day has been horrible," Carl sobbed between grasps for tissue after tissue. "I woke up so exhausted to start with. I already had an emotional hangover from a fight my wife and I had last night. Plus, it didn't get any better once I sat down to read the morning news. This current administration is horrific. I can't believe how cruel and callous they are." Carl paused for a moment, took a deep breath, and continued.

"My commute was frustrating, too. Rainy days are hard enough, but with these tourists who don't know how to walk down the street properly with umbrellas, I almost had my eye poked out, twice! It was so hard not to yell at someone. I know no one was purposely trying to hurt me, but it was so frustrating! Why is it raining so much this time of year, anyway? Shouldn't it be snowing instead? Why isn't anyone taking climate change seriously?"

Carl kept on, saying he dreaded having to return to his office with its open floorplan. He wanted to run and hide and felt only like sobbing. He wondered if some of the fear and dread he was feeling also had to do with an upcoming family reunion, which he thought lasted far too long, was far too loud, and just far too much! He wanted to know what was wrong with him and why everyone else seemed to deal with life so easily. Why couldn't he buck up and why was he just so damn sensitive?

Carl's story illustrates what a challenging day can look like for highly sensitive people—overwhelmed and frustrated by a day that's just too much. Not only do we experience the world at a higher and more intense frequency because of our finely tuned nervous systems, but we often feel a deep sense of shame and self-criticism because we often do not meet societal and familial expectations. Our needs are not always mirrored or honored.

In my clinical work, I find many males, especially, arrive at therapy suffering from anger management issues, substance abuse, depression, and anxiety. Through courageous work, many learn that they are also highly sensitive. It seems to be more difficult for the men and boys I have seen than for the women to express or regulate intense emotions and responses, perhaps because of social constructs. This difficulty also seems to be true for those who experienced childhood trauma.

Many of us highly sensitive people can relate to Carl's frustration and experiences. Ideally, we want to learn how to channel our sensitivity into action and direction to help ourselves get through our bad days, soothe our sensitive nervous systems, process our "big" feelings, and move on.

A recent study found that though highly sensitive people struggle with our own highly sensitive nature, we tend to be less affected by cultural norms and pressures. We tend not to blindly accept what culture dictates. As Elaine Aron said at the 2019 Highly Sensitive Therapist retreat, "Despite culture, highly sensitive people see things how they are!"

A majority of the highly sensitive people I work with report having difficulties in social interactions as well as in relationships with family, friends, and romantic partners. Some struggle with choosing a profession or keeping up with the pace and demands of their job.

Overstimulation, whether environmental, social, or emotional, is also quite common among highly sensitive people. This may be especially true with my personal experience because my office is located in New York City. Just getting on the subway, where we are bombarded with a barrage of people, sights, sounds, and smells, can be a struggle for many highly sensitive people.

Highly sensitive people have played a vital part in both ancient and modern societies. Studies show that the world needs highly sensitive people for their physical, emotional, and spiritual survival skills. Our innate and responsive systems offer important advantages in hunting, gathering, or seeking a mate. We know the shortcuts, how to rewire, and how to create beauty and find balance. Because of our finely tuned systems, we can take in more sensory information see details and nuances that many less sensitive people cannot (Belsky and Pluess 2009).

Additionally, many highly sensitive people play the role of "priestly advisor" (Aron 2011). With our keen attention to detail, deep intuition, and creative and innovative nature, many of us become the one that others seek out for advice, guidance, or emotional support.

Carl, my client, was able to turn his day around. Before we continued with the session, he asked if we could do a quick grounding exercise we had practiced previously to help soothe his agitated nervous system. When Carl focused on his breath, he began to relax. After a few minutes, Carl was able to process the feelings evoked by his difficult day and begin to plan his evening.

He decided to get through his workday as gently as possible, and then talk with his wife about his thoughts on the disagreement they had had the previous night. He also planned to call one of his siblings to discuss ways to set firm boundaries for the upcoming family reunion he was somewhat dreading and to talk to this sibling about a new business venture that might help him get out of his current, open-office working environment. As Carl continued to honor and process his feelings, his tears dried and his face relaxed and softened.

By the time Carl was ready to head out my office door, he had been able to engage in our usual end-of-session ritual of exchanging bad "dad jokes" and making old *South Park* references. (Healing comes in many forms!) He left with an exhale of relief and a plan in place, feeling strong, empowered, and most important, himself.

In this book, I hope to help you discover and honor your incredible HSP trait. I encourage you to work with the parts that feel difficult, draining, and challenging. This work will help you get through days or experiences that feel overwhelming, just like we saw with our friend Carl.

# THE WISDOM OF MR. ROGERS: DEVELOPING COMPASSION FOR YOUR PAST AND PRESENT

I am certain, because of his beautiful and unmistakable compassion and unparalleled understanding of the human condition, that Fred Rogers was a highly sensitive person. In the 2018 documentary *Won't You Be My Neighbor?*, Rogers passionately expressed the need and importance for both children and adults to be with and process their feelings, even the "big" and difficult ones.

Many highly sensitive people, myself included, have unfortunately been made to feel like a burden to those around us. We are told repeatedly that our feelings are too big or too much. Some of my clients learned to suppress their feelings to survive emotionally, or because they were taught that full expression of their emotions, deep thoughts, worries, or longings, were weird, wrong, or dangerous.

Some HSP children are confused by their deep connection to nature, plants, or animals, or strong reaction to a change in the school schedule or the weather. One of my clients, Tom, reported that he used to hide how much he loved the family dog because he worried about seeming weak or silly to his older brothers. Another highly sensitive client, Yukiko, reported that after each school semester, she would experience grief at the semester's conclusion because the enjoyable time she had spent learning and socializing with her peers was over.

Many highly sensitive children suffer from low self-esteem and feel that something is deeply wrong with them, or that they should be able to "handle more." I remember several times as a child, during a sleepover or watching a movie with friends, hiding my sadness or fear. I distinctly remember wanting to cry at a movie but being deeply afraid to because I didn't want to seem weird.

Though the childhood difficulties and traumas of highly sensitive people are not the fault of their highly sensitive nature, a highly sensitive child can be more prone to experience the symptoms of trauma as a result of an unhealthy relationship, attachment, or incident. If lucky enough to experience a happy, stress-reduced childhood, as well as the benefit and privilege of an attuned parent, a highly sensitive child can thrive and become a well-balanced, well-regulated adult. Unfortunately, when highly sensitive children have the opposite experience, they are likely to experience stronger negative effects of a neglectful or abusive parent or a traumatic childhood than those not as sensitive.

How can a highly sensitive person heal from childhood trauma? Is it possible for a highly sensitive person who has experienced a tough childhood to thrive as an adult? Can an individual who has been diagnosed with PTSD, depression, and anxiety because of their traumatic experiences learn to manage their symptoms and fully live their life?

Because I have had the joy and privilege of doing my own healing work as a highly sensitive person, and through counseling other highly sensitive individuals in my practice for over 10 years, I can answer all those questions with a resounding and ecstatic YES! If the client and therapist or healer are attuned, motivated, compassionate, and patient, a highly sensitive person can absolutely heal their wounds from the past and better manage their present. Because of our ability for depth and deep emotional intelligence, highly sensitive people tend to be quite good at contributing to our own healing journeys. The empathy, compassion, and attunement we so naturally give others can also be turned inward (sometimes with a bit of help and support), and we can benefit from this love and quality of presence.

## TRAIT OR TRAUMA?

One of the most challenging, but useful, exercises I do with clients helps them identify differences between their trauma symptoms and their innate highly sensitive traits. Anxious thoughts, fear of social situations, and over-stimulation (also called *hyperarousal*) can be present in both situations.

By developing more awareness and consciousness about our environmental, social, and relational habits, we can help identify current traumatic symptoms that may be hidden, or folded into, our innate traits. With this identification, we can create more consciousness and choice in how we want to relate to the world and in our relationships while embracing our authentic sensitive nature.

This questionnaire will help you explore and assess traumatic symptoms that might exist alongside your highly sensitive traits. I have also listed common HSP characteristics and common signs of trauma. There are no right or wrong answers, just a gentle exploration of the unique makeup of you. These questions are a starting place to consider your own trauma history and to see if perhaps you possess some symptoms of trauma you might not be aware of. Many highly sensitive people and humans in general are sometimes unaware that they have experienced trauma and are displaying symptoms of it. Uncovering and working with trauma symptoms while honoring and developing the strengths of the HSP trait will help you heal. This work will also help you honor your beautiful sensitive nature.

HSP traits: depth of processing, overstimulation, emotional responsiveness, awareness of subtle stimuli, deep connection to arts and nature, a rich complex inner life, feelings of greater connection to spirituality.

Trauma symptoms include loss of connection to mind and body, hyperperception of threat, overstimulation, constriction in mind and body in preparing for a threat, dissociation and denial, feelings of helplessness, immobility, and freezing. To identify these symptoms, answer these 24 questions.

1. When you walk into a room, do you ever scan it to assess for safety or comfort? (looking for possible threatening people or situations, poor air quality [too hot/cold/crowded/empty])

2. Do you ever feel "peopled out" or pay attention to the "vibe" you get from someone?

3. Have you ever had a strong response (positive or negative) to someone you just met?

4. Do you ever feel like your sensitive trait can get in the way of experiencing things that look interesting or exciting to you?

5. Do you ever have days where *everything* seems like too much and you want to crawl into a hole never to be seen again?

6. Have you experienced a major trauma in your life in the past or recently (death, loss, breakup, natural disaster)?

7. If yes to number six: After the traumatic incident, did you find you were more sensitive to your emotions and environment?

8. Do you have any sensitivities to doctor's offices or hospitals (sights, smells, etc.)? Do you get overwhelmed when you have to go to the doctor?

9. Do you feel like your parents misunderstood and rejected your sensitive nature?

10. Do you feel your "authentic self" was discouraged?

11. Do you feel emotions were restricted in your house growing up? (For example, it was okay to display anger but not fear; it was okay to be happy but not ecstatic.)

12. Did you ever hide your emotional reaction to something because of fear of being ridiculed, punished, or shamed by loved ones for being too sensitive or emotional?

13. Do you ever worry you are inherently "bad" or "worthless," or even that if people knew the "real you" they would no longer like you?

14. Has anyone in your personal or professional life ever "weaponized" your emotional responses or sensitivity to demean or assert power over you?

15. Are you very good with "difficult" people because you are able to read them and anticipate their needs and demands?

16. Are "mistakes" either at work, home, or social situations ever incredibly painful or even fear-provoking for you?

17. Does being hungry or suffering from any other kind of physical discomfort ever make you agitated or even anxious?

18. Do you get overwhelmed with your self-care needs?

19. Do you ever have trouble sleeping?

20. Do you ever enter an unknown situation worried your sensitive needs will not be met?

21. Are you always well prepared? (Have a purse, bag, or trunk filled with "just in case" items?)

22. Do you have any self-soothing habits or addictions (for example, smoking, eating, shopping, sex) that help you cope with the world around you?

23. Does your family system have intergenerational trauma from within the family or on a larger society scale? (Intergenerational trauma is passed down through generations and may include emotional or physical abuse, sudden loss of a family member, war, or a natural disaster. It can appear through behavior, attachment styles, belief systems, and, as discovered through the study of epigenetics, even in our DNA.)

24. Is avoidance of people and situations one of your main coping strategies for your high sensitivity?

If you answered "yes" to most of the questions, especially numbers 1, 6, 8, 10, 11, 12, 13, 15, 16, 18, 22, 23 and 24, there is a strong likelihood you are displaying symptoms of trauma. The tools, skills, and strategies we will cover later in the book can help manage and contain some of the symptoms you might be experiencing. If you are in therapy, this would be helpful information to share with your therapist.

# CORE SKILLS FOR THE HIGHLY SENSITIVE PERSON

This section focuses on the sensitive core skills which are a set of tools and practices to assist you across all areas of your highly sensitive life. These skills will also help support and strengthen the strategies discussed later in this book.

Every human being has what is called a "window of tolerance" for environmental and emotional stimuli. This term, originally coined by psychologist Dr. Daniel Siegel (1999), indicates the level at which life is tolerable enough to be able to manage physical and emotional responses so that we can feel and respond in a healthy way to the needs of our mind and body. We highly sensitive people take in more sensory information than those less sensitive and tend to have a stronger response to negative or traumatic symptoms because of our finely tuned nervous systems. Unfortunately, we are more likely to experience nervous system overwhelm or be kicked out of our window of tolerance and become overstimulated.

There are two ways in which a human can respond to overstimulation: activation into a state of fight-or-flight with feelings of anxiety, anger, or overwhelm; or freezing with feelings of numbness, dissociation, or being spaced out.

During these responses, the brain's prefrontal cortex—responsible for a higher level of thinking, reasoning, and logic—shuts down, and our innate survival instincts kick in. Though designed to help us survive an immediate threat, our sensitive nervous systems may set off this alert system when we are overstimulated or in response to a past trauma.

Regardless of the source of your automatic responses, discovering your "window of tolerance" and learning the sensitive core skills presented in this book will be a tool for developing a deeper consciousness of your highly sensitive nature to respond to and soothe your sensitive nervous system. With practice, your sensitive superpowers can emerge!

## Self-advocacy/Self-parenting

Self-advocacy is a vital skill for highly sensitive people. Because the outside world often does not understand our sensitive needs and nature, we sometimes have to ask ourselves or others to make adjustments to our environments or relationships. Think of self-advocacy as self-parenting.

Highly sensitive people are more likely to respond negatively to a parent not attuned to their sensitive needs and to respond positively to a parent who is attuned to their needs. The more we learn about what we need to live and thrive, the more we can communicate our needs. We can become the attentive parent we might not have had. Very simply, we can ask for what we need or want!

### Self-parenting/Advocacy Skill Set

- **Ask** for what you need to feel comfortable, safe, and grounded.

- **Receive** what you need to feel comfortable, safe, and grounded.

- **Develop and nurture** self-curiosity. Ask yourself the simple questions: How am I today? How am I feeling? How does my body feel? How does my soul feel?

- **Practice** self-compassion. Acknowledge any difficulty and offer yourself warm wishes that things will get better.

- **Bring awareness** to your internal dialogue or how you speak to yourself. Ask: How am I talking to myself? Am I being kind or critical?

### Self-advocacy/Self-parenting in Practice

We must learn to request accommodations when we need them! Imagine getting into an Uber or Lyft with the radio blasting talk radio and the heat turned up to an uncomfortable level. You immediately notice your body's response to the heat and sound. You acknowledge this discomfort within yourself and gently ask the driver to turn down the radio. He happily complies with the request. You crack the window to let in some cool air. You then take a few moments to readjust and check in with yourself again. You notice you are more comfortable now. You have taken care of your discomfort!

Just as an attuned parent would adjust their child's environment if they needed it, you must fulfill your needs.

## Developing Awareness of Overstimulation

When we are overstimulated and overwhelmed, we are less likely to access our highly sensitive superpowers and greater gifts. This overstimulation doesn't just happen in negative situations. Positive events or circumstances can also leave the highly sensitive person feeling overwhelmed. Developing awareness of overstimulation, then, is an important sensitive core skill in taking care of ourselves. This awareness also helps us connect better with our authentic selves and true likes or dislikes.

Many highly sensitive people, and most people in general, are not taught the tools to mindfully notice and observe their own physical and emotional states. Use this skill set to help guide your observations.

## Skill Set

- **Observe the quality of mind.** What does overstimulation in the mind feel like? Happy? Sad? Nervous? Angry? What *quality* of thoughts are present?

- **Observe the quality of body.** What does overstimulation in the body feel like? Tense? Tingling? Coursing? Buzzing? What *quality* of sensations are present?

- **Observe the cues.** What are the cues in the mind and body to over-stimulation? Can you notice them without judging or wishing them away?

Common cues for overstimulation in the mind: racing, repetitive anxious thoughts (rumination) playing out anxiety-inducing scenarios; imagining "the worst" possible outcome; angry or sad internal dialogue.

Common cues for overstimulation in the body: tightness in the face, neck, shoulders or stomach; clenched fist or jaw; excess energy in the body, feeling fidgety, unable to rest or sit still; stomach clenching or upset; rapid heartbeat; shallow breathing; feeling too hot or cold; feeling "stuck" or "frozen."

## In Practice

You walk into a packed grocery store to pick up a few items. As you move around the store, you begin to notice and observe the quality of your mind and body. Your mind is filled with angry, nervous, or overwhelmed thoughts. "Why are there so many damn people in this store? Why can't some of them stay home? What if they don't have the items I need? Why are there so many choices? Why do we need this many types of cereal? How do I choose?" You also begin to notice sensations in your body. Your hands tighten on the handle of the basket you are carrying and they begin to sweat. Your jaw tenses. Your stomach feels slightly queasy. Sweat builds on your upper lip. The store suddenly feels too hot and stuffy. You've got to get out of here, fast!

You have observed you are overstimulated and may need to employ the soothing skills discussed later in this chapter.

- An example of positive overstimulation: I attended the Women's March in New York City in 2016, just after the US presidential inauguration. When my friends and I arrived to a packed Second Avenue in Midtown—full of pink hats, amazingly clever signs, and emotionally charged chants—I found myself speechless and frozen at what I was witnessing. I was overstimulated but also in awe and feeling lucky to be a part of it. I could barely move or speak. I noticed I just kept looking around unable to connect with what I was feeling. I felt my eyes widen, chest tighten, and mind race. (I will tell you how I got regulated later in the chapter.)

## Developing Awareness of a Regulated and Calm Nervous System

Recognizing and observing your nervous system when it is calm and regulated will help you rewire, which encourages a faster recovery in those moments when you are feeling overstimulated and overwhelmed. We humans are excellent at knowing when we feel "bad," but feeling "good" often goes unnoticed.

### Skill Set

- **Stop to notice** when the mind and body feel calm and regulated. These are the times you can attain higher and more sophisticated levels of thinking.

- **Recall** a time you felt at your "best" to help you notice the calm now. Drawing from memories of calm and strength will help bring your focus to these feelings in the present moment.

- **Bring presence** to your situation. Focus on the breath to help focus your mind on what's happening now. Pay attention to the cues the mind provides when you are calm and your nervous system is regulated.

#### COMMON CUES

Common cues for a regulated, calm nervous system include "flowing" thoughts and the the ability to think critically, even under pressure or stress;

the ability to think creatively and expansively; allowance for mistakes, or "imperfect" or "bad" ideas or thoughts; and thinking before speaking or acting on something.

Common cues for a regulated, calm nervous system in terms of the body include: sensing less or no tension in the muscles; moving with ease, grace, and balance; feeling comfortable, not too hot or cold.

### Practice: Developing Awareness of a Regulated, Calm Nervous System

At the end of a "good" day—one in which you've felt calm and regulated—take a few minutes to practice a "body scan." Begin at your head or feet, whichever feels best for you. Simply observe your body's sensations from one end to the other. Take a basic inventory, without judgment, simply seeing what is there.

What sensations are there in this moment? Any areas that feel relaxed? What temperatures do you notice in each part as you scan? After you've gone through your whole body, take a few moments to reflect on your experiences. It can be helpful to record these observations in a journal, your phone, or whatever works best.

## Learning to Soothe: Working with Our "Self-Cleaning Oven"

Yes, it's true. Highly sensitive people can become overstimulated. Luckily, though, our finely tuned nervous system can learn to regulate itself, much like a self-cleaning oven can get itself clean. This "self-cleaning" is a learned skill that begins with noticing when we are feeling overstimulated (see "Developing Awareness of Overstimulation" on page 16). That's when we hit the self-cleaning button, entering calming and soothing mode. Knowing when and how to enter this mode is an incredible tool for a highly sensitive person and is especially helpful if we have also experienced trauma that sparks hyper- or hypo-arousal.

### Skill Set

- **Calm and ground** the mind and body when overstimulated.

- **Regulate** the mind and body.

### In Practice

Though there are many tools that help regulate the nervous system (e.g., meditation, deep breathing, somatic experiencing), the simplest and most effective is to literally get on the ground. Our highly sensitive nervous systems have a deep connection to the earth, and to gravity itself, and we can utilize this connection to help soothe our overstimulated nervous systems. When you notice you are overstimulated, try to find a way to make contact with the earth, either by sitting or lying down. If you can find some nature to sit or lie on, absolutely go for it! If you can take your shoes off, even better! As you begin to make contact with the earth, and the delicious gravity that is holding you, take a few moments to regulate your breathing from your belly. Take as long as you need, sitting or lying until you feel some relief. If you are unable to sit or lie down, simply bring your awareness to your feet and how they feel making contact with the earth.

Remember my experience of being overstimulated at the Women's March? After first noticing the cues my mind and body were giving me that I was overwhelmed, I stepped aside to ground myself. After a few deep belly breaths, finding my feet on the ground, and telling a friend how overstimulated I felt, I was able to march and participate, fully present.

## Developing Awareness of Emotions: Naming, Allowing, and Processing Feelings

Because highly sensitive people have greater access to our emotional landscapes and experience emotions at a higher frequency, we can acknowledge our feelings more readily than those less sensitive. After this acknowledgement, we'll likely want to employ calming and soothing techniques or just be with our feelings.

### Skill Set

- **Observe** all feelings, without judgment, as they arise.

- **Give** yourself space to process feelings.

- **Acknowledge** your right as a human being to have all feelings, "good" or "bad."

- **Remember** feelings are just feelings. You don't always have to act on them; they can just be.

## In Practice

Soon after I discovered I was a highly sensitive person, I attended a training that focused on trauma and included a video of individuals sharing their trauma and explaining their healing process. I was incredibly moved and felt that old familiar lump in my throat when I want to cry but am trying to hold back. I took a deep breath, looked around at the room of therapists, and recognized nothing bad was going to happen to me if I shed a few tears. So, I cried. I let my tears fall. I sniffed, I wiped, I heaved. I allowed myself to feel my own feelings and to express them. The old painful lump was gone. I didn't cry because I was weak or broken. I cried because I had been deeply moved by what I was observing. And it was okay.

## Honoring and Responding to Truth and Justice

One of the principal hallmarks of the highly sensitive person is the deep desire to honor truth and justice within our own internal or external worlds. This can also be an important skill to develop when thinking of a job, career, vocation, or calling.

### Skill Set

- **Honor** the need for truth and justice in the world

- **Respect** that as a highly sensitive person you have a gift for "seeing the truth" even if others don't. We are the canaries in the coal mine!

- **Communicate** to others in a respectful way about your need for truth and justice.

- **Soothe and calm** yourself when others don't understand or see what you see.

- **Take action** for truth and justice for yourself or your community, if needed.

### In Practice

Honoring and responding to a need for truth and justice can be exercised in both our professional and personal lives. Professionally, we can choose a vocation or career that helps the world and humanity such as therapist, activist, or volunteer. In our personal lives, this need for truth and justice may appear as speaking the truth in our relationships even if it brings discomfort to others. For example, a client of mine was concerned about her girlfriend's alcohol use but was afraid to tell her because she thought it would upset her and they would break up. After processing her fear, she was able to tell the truth of her experience to her partner, which actually assisted her in creating a healthier lifestyle and, in turn, relationship.

## Honoring and Developing Joy and Creativity

Being aware of and connecting to what brings joy, creativity, and flow is especially important for a highly sensitive person. This awareness nourishes our highly sensitive selves and brings us calm. It is also vital to our sensitive life force.

It is easy for the highly sensitive child to be discouraged from developing the spark of joy and creativity by well-intentioned caregivers who told us to "calm down" or "be quiet" when our highly sensitive selves got excited or thrilled about something. "Too much" creativity (e.g., coloring outside the lines), too, can be seen as a negative and discouraged.

### Skill Set

- **Recognize** "flow." The deep concentration of flow can happen with another person while creating art or when in nature.

- **See** your mind and body states when thrilled or excited.

- **Allow** yourself to express happiness.

### In Practice

I am literally practicing this as I am sitting here typing this paragraph. I note the ease of my fingers across the keyboard, the flow of my thoughts, and the soft hum in my belly. I connect the body sensations with a thought as I inhale . . . mmmm . . . I am enjoying this writing flow. I am . . . exhale . . . ahhhh . . . feels nice . . . I'll keep going. . . .

Another fabulous place to practice is at an event, perhaps a concert of an artist you love. As you listen to the music, notice how it feels as it enters your ears and flows through your body. Are you smiling, laughing, screaming in musical ecstasy? Perhaps you are! Enjoy!

# Setting and Tolerating Boundaries

Developing this skill set is vital for any highly sensitive person's interpersonal relationships. Setting healthy and tolerable boundaries for work and personal relationships not only creates clear rules and expectations for a highly sensitive person's relationships but also provides protection from unhealthy situations or relationships that may be harmful, unproductive, or dysfunctional. Setting boundaries at work or with friends and family will also be discussed in later chapters. Generally, without good boundaries, we have to manage discomfort with ourselves and others.

## Skill Set

- **Be aware** of personal and professional boundaries.

- **Note** when personal or professional boundaries have been crossed or violated.

- **Acknowledge** your right, highly sensitive or not, to have boundaries. Always!

- **Recognize** that boundaries exist for a reason. They are the rules and structure of our world and relationships to keep us safe and protected.

## In Practice

We exercise this skill when we make a behavior change request of a loved one, co-worker, or even a stranger. For example, my client Mariella, had two co-workers who would constantly come to her desk during the day to chat or ask advice. Though flattered, Mariella began to notice that her co-workers' constant need for attention was emotionally draining and also prevented her from getting her own work done. Upon processing her feelings in session, she recognized she wanted and needed to create a boundary. Mariella, using her gift of high sensitivity to recognize how she wanted to deliver her message, was able to successfully craft a simple verbal request to both women in a firm, yet gracious, way that she was unable to talk at that time and could they reconnect later? The request was successfully heard, and Mariella was able to get back to work.

## Reframing Difficult Situations

Reframing is the re-evaluation of a situation, event, thought, or opinion. This can be helpful when we are feeling helpless in a situation or have little control over our environment. Because we sometimes cannot adjust a situation or a person to our liking, reframing, re-examining, or renaming a situation can help increase the "window of tolerance" for an uncomfortable circumstance or relationship. I find this skill to be especially useful when dealing with sensory overstimulation (e.g., lights, sounds, smells).

### Skill Set

- **Re-examine** a difficult situation, especially one in which there is little control.

- **Allow** another point of view for a difficult situation.

- **Make light** or find humor in a situation.

### In Practice

The New York City subway system is a fabulous place to practice reframing a situation where we have little control. A number of sensory overwhelm issues can occur inside those little metal rockets zooming under the city all day long. Sometimes you are able to switch cars or wait for the next train, but sometimes you just gotta get to work and must manage your overwhelm. Many of my HSP clients as well as myself are very sensitive to the ever abundant smells in the subway. One rushed morning I jumped onto the 7 train and after the doors closed quickly behind me, I was enveloped in a smell I can only describe as flaming hot garbage with a side of rotting hot dogs. The train was packed, and I was late and unable to escape the situation, so I tapped into my wonderful HSP trait of creativity and ingenuity (after plugging my nose and pulling a scarf over half my face) and invented this game that I invite you to play.

Let us play . . . (in an announcer's voice) . . . WHAT'S . . . THAT . . . SMELL??!!!!!!! (ding ding ding . . . lights, sounds, glitter, and lasers, etc. . . .) The game instantly begins when we smell our first smell. Rather than get bogged down with thoughts and sensations about all the ways we are suffering, get curious about that smell. What's the smell's story? Where did it come from? Can we find the originator of the smell? Does it have any relatives? Does it have an Instagram account? How long has the smell been here? What does this smell want?

I know this technique seems silly but sometimes laughing at a ridiculous situation in which we are stuck can reduce our suffering and overwhelm until we can reach our destination.

# TAKEAWAYS

Highly sensitive people have sensory processing sensitivity, defined by four primary indicators: depth of processing, over-stimulation, emotional responsiveness, and awareness of subtle stimuli. It is not a diagnosis or condition but an innate trait in some humans and animals.

Highly sensitive people can be introverted, extroverted, or a mixture of both. Though we tend to identify as deeply empathic, not all of us are. We can be any gender, sexual orientation, or from any culture.

Repeat after me: There is nothing wrong with me! Rather, a general lack of understanding surrounding different ways individuals process emotions is actually the problem. To thrive, the world needs highly sensitive people.

To embark upon a healing journey and honor your sensitive nature, you must consider your history, especially your trauma history if you have one.

The nine sensitive core skills help with overwhelm, regulating your nervous system, and honoring your highly sensitive nature.

For the "Skill Set" sections, I invite you to find opportunities to practice these when the stakes are low. Because some of the strategies might be uncomfortable or foreign to you, be sure to move at your own pace. Don't "jump into the deep end" too soon.

Highly sensitive people are naturally talented at healing others as well as themselves. Consider your highly sensitive nature a fabulous gift as you embark upon the path of embracing your authentic self.

# CHAPTER TWO
# Higher-Frequency Living: Everyday Life

Because of the fast pace of today's world, highly sensitive people (and I think many human beings at this point) are often pressured to work and live at a speed that is overwhelming and overstimulating for them. Additionally, many highly sensitive people struggle and judge themselves for feeling frazzled and chronically exhausted. We have been taught, implicitly or explicitly, that our natural responses to the world are simply too much or wrong.

Many highly sensitive people struggle with issues of time: being on time and how to properly pace and manage their day. We can hit the snooze button more than our less sensitive peers or struggle to get out of our houses or apartments to begin our day. Not uncommonly, many of us are exhausted or frazzled before we even start our daily tasks.

Even our email inboxes can be overwhelming and overstimulating. Upon clicking the seemingly harmless and adorable little envelope on our iPhones we are plunged into a world of immediacy, panic, and 24/7 news cycles.

Urgent! Breaking! Last chance! Emails and ads from stores inform us that we are milliseconds away from missing the best deals ever! Even emails I get from psychotherapy and therapy websites and training centers send repetitive marketing emails with headings such as, "You have one hour left to sign up for this training!"

This chapter looks at how to discover your optimal levels of stimulation in your day-to-day life and how to work with rather than against your highly sensitive nervous system.

# YOUR OPTIMAL LEVEL OF STIMULATION: DETERMINING YOUR UNIQUE HIGHLY SENSITIVE STYLE

As we begin to honor our HSP trait, we want to become aware of the type of highly sensitive people we are. I've outlined the five types here. As you read through them, see which you most closely relate to, keeping in mind it will likely be a combination. This deeper assessment will help you understand which sensitive core skills will best serve you.

**EMOTIONAL:** The emotional highly sensitive person is the type with which I, and likely most therapists and healers, identify. This type typically develops deep bonds and, like empaths, feels not only their own emotions and physical sensations deeply but sometimes those of other humans, animals, or other living creatures. So, if someone we are close to is nervous or upset, we might pick up and feel these same emotions even though these emotions do not belong to us. Psychosomatic responses to emotions are also common among this type and might include sweaty palms, rapid heartbeat, or uneasy stomach.

**IMAGINATIONAL:** These highly sensitive people are most likely to become writers, poets, filmmakers, comedians, or any type of artistic revolutionary that helps reflect and enhance our world. Because this imaginational type prefers to live in the subconscious or within created fantasy or dream worlds (who can blame them?), these highly sensitive people tend to have a lower tolerance for reality and the demands of everyday life.

**INTELLECTUAL:** Intellectual highly sensitive people are deep, reflective thinkers. Those of this type tend to have a knack for vividly recalling information, which also makes them skilled problem solvers. With a deep desire for truth and logic, they can become frustrated with themselves, others, and the world at large when things don't make sense to them. As children, they are more likely to ask "But why?" until they are satisfied.

**PSYCHOMOTOR:** A strong drive and high energy levels are hallmarks of the psychomotor highly sensitive person. These individuals love intense physical activity and are sometimes, though not always, gifted athletes. Their love for sports also plays into a deep need for competition. Aside from their desire to move their bodies at a fast pace, their minds and speech can also run at a higher pace, sometimes in a way that does not serve them. As a response to this speed and possible overstimulation, these highly sensitive people can sometimes develop nervous or self-soothing habits such as nail biting.

**SENSUAL:** These highly sensitive people exist in a world where all five senses are greatly enhanced, often providing extreme pleasure but also overstimulation. This type may experience music, art, and food or anything that appeals to the senses as ecstatic or spiritual. These heightened sensitivities can lead to issues with food or "picky eating" during childhood. As adults, these highly sensitive people can be more prone to food, sex, or other sense-fulfilling addictions than the other types or those less sensitive. Those of this type need downtime to recover their highly tuned senses.

## High Sensation–Seeking Highly Sensitive People:

According to Elaine Aron about 30 percent of all highly sensitive people, regardless of type, seek high sensation. This means they draw more enjoyment from high-sensory activities such as loud, soul-enriching live music and crave novelty, variety, and new and exciting experiences.

I personally identify as a high sensation–seeking highly sensitive person as well as an emotional one. Though I love exciting and novel experiences, I always need downtime afterward to process and rest my senses.

# Learn Your Tipping/Overstimulation Point

Key for us highly sensitive people is to be aware of our tipping or overstimulation point, when the nervous system has clearly had enough and we need rest (see "Developing Awareness of Overstimulation," page 16). Developing awareness of the conditions that cause us to be physically or emotionally overstimulated can empower us to have more effective and efficient day-to-day interactions. Here are some common sources of overstimulation. Different people will be triggered by different types of stimuli.

**EMOTIONAL:** Humans, highly sensitive or not, are emotional beings. Those of us who identify as empaths must pay particular attention to our emotional states and know that we are more prone to becoming overwhelmed than other HSP types. We highly sensitive people who identify with emotional overstimulation must absolutely protect our emotional energy by creating and setting boundaries. Practicing the sensitive core skills of "Developing Awareness of Emotions: Naming, Allowing, and Processing Feelings" (see page 20) and "Developing Awareness of a Regulated and Calm Nervous System" (see page 18) is also very helpful for emotional highly sensitive people. Though we tend to lead with our hearts, and this is beautiful, we must know when we have reached our heart's capacity and turn to soothing. We must be aware of "psychic or energy vampires" or "trauma vomiters" (see pages 46–47).

**IMAGINATIONAL:** Having a rich, imaginative life is amazing, and especially good for creativity, but it is also a hindrance for some highly sensitive people. Be sure to check in with yourself to ensure you aren't spending too much time in your imagination, or in imaginary worlds. The skill of "Setting and Tolerating Boundaries" (see page 23) will likely be helpful. Make sure the amount of time you spend in your imagination serves your overall well-being. This might mean taking a break from a really engrossing book or putting down the video game console to take a walk outside. For imaginational highly sensitive people, the skill of "Honoring and Developing Joy and Creativity" (see page 22) may be particularly beneficial.

**INTELLECTUAL:** Information can be overstimulating for a highly sensitive person. The intellectual highly sensitive person might be pulled in to as much information as their attention allows. Setting boundaries or time limits on how much you watch, read, or research might help. Also, be compassionate toward others and yourself if there is a topic you or others don't know as much about. "Honoring and Responding to Truth and Justice" (see page 21) might be a key skill to refine. "Reframing Difficult Situations" (see page 24) might also be a good tool to navigate those people who prove to be difficult to educate despite our best efforts.

**PSYCHOMOTOR:** Be mindful of sensations within your body and what these are communicating to you. If driven to seek out physical activities, don't push yourself beyond your physical limits. "Self-advocacy/Self-parenting" (see page 15) and "Setting and Tolerating Boundaries" (see page 23) might be good skills to practice here because you may need to advocate for rest when needed. "Learning to Soothe: Working with Our 'Self-Cleaning Oven'" (see page 19) may be helpful as well.

**SENSUAL:** Anything sensory such as foods, smells, loud noises, and lights can be a source of overstimulation. Be aware of addictions that might emerge as a result of your overstimulation. Also, look for opportunities for downtime to soothe your senses. The core skill of "Learning to Soothe: Working with Our 'Self-Cleaning Oven'" (see page 19) can bring calm to the senses and quiet to the nervous system.

## Best Day Ever: An Imaginative Practice for Optimal Stimulation

In your journal, or wherever you like, write about your "perfect day" in terms of your own optimal stimulation. What would you see, smell, hear, taste, and touch?

Break down your day into three categories: morning, midday, and night. For each time period, list what your ideal sensory environment would look, smell, sound, and taste like.

Example:

Morning:

- I see the bright sunshine beaming through my window.

- I touch my dog's fur as I pet and snuggle him in bed before I get up for the day.

- I smell the coffee brewing that I set up last night.

- I hear the classical music I put on for myself as soon as I woke up.

- I taste my spectacular coffee along with my favorite breakfast.

After you have written about your ideal day, play with some possibilities, and see how you can incorporate more pleasurable sensory moments into your daily life. Though our days cannot always be perfect, it is possible to create more pleasurable sensory moments in our day-to-day lives.

## Tips and Tools for the High Sensation–Seeking Highly Sensitive Person

*If you are unsure if you are also high sensation–seeking, take the HSS quiz on Elaine Aron's website, HSPerson.com.*

For those of us who identify as high sensation–seeking, we must walk a fine line as we crave novelty and excitement as much as we crave quiet and downtime. Become familiar with what kind of balance serves your nervous system best. We can tend toward burnout because of our need to seek out highly stimulating experiences.

- If you know you will be participating in a possibly overwhelming experience, plan recovery or downtime for yourself afterward. Example: Travel home alone, rather than with friends, from a loud, crowded concert to let your nervous system settle with the gift of quiet.

- As a high sensation–seeking highly sensitive person, you might tend to "pile on" stimulating experiences and then overschedule yourself with exciting or pleasurable activities. If you notice you are feeling frequently rushed and overwhelmed, consider scheduling more breaks or downtime into your day.

- Develop awareness and understanding that people might have difficulty fully understanding what they see as contradictory traits. Because we can appear as a mix of introversion and extroversion—loud and intense sometimes but quiet and contempla-tive at others—high sensation–seeking highly sensitive people may need to educate others about our preferences at certain times.

# EVERYDAY ACTIVITIES AND INTERACTIONS

Though all human beings have to manage their time, highly sensitive people can have an especially difficult time doing so, especially when others are relying on our timeliness. This is due to our depth of processing and ten-dency to become overstimulated by our environment, especially if it involves rushing or having to be somewhere at a certain time.

We can also have difficulty creating routines and schedules that suit our highly sensitive natures, especially if our caregivers did not teach us this skill when we were children. Life circumstances or an inability to honor our individual needs, create boundaries, or say no to requests made of us can all contribute to these difficulties. Many highly sensitive people find themselves taking care of others' needs before taking care of their own.

What follows in this chapter are strategies to help manage time. The sensitive core skills of "Self-advocacy/Self-parenting" (see page 15), "Developing Awareness of Overstimulation" (see page 16), "Developing Awareness of Emotions: Naming, Allowing, and Processing Feelings" (see page 20), "Learning to Soothe: Working with Our 'Self-Cleaning Oven'" (see page 19), and "Setting and Tolerating Boundaries" (see page 23) will be particularly useful to help master these strategies.

## Working with Transitions and Time

- Keep time a part of your consciousness as much as possible. Wear a watch, set alarms, and keep a clock that is easy to spot in every room so you can stay aware of the time if you need to arrive at a destination at a certain time.

- Overestimate how long it actually takes you to get ready and leave the house, even if it seems silly. I will generally give myself two or three times the amount of time I need to get myself out the door. This extra time leaves room for me to move at a pace where I don't feel rushed.

- Change your clothing or shoes when you transition from one activity to the next. As highly sensitive people, we can sometimes struggle to move from one activity to the next. I suspect this may be due to our brains' tendency to process experiences deeply. I imagine our brains are still processing an experience, even if the clock dictates it's time to move on to our next task. By changing our clothing or shoes, we are reminding the body through movement and sensations of new materials that we are moving to the next activity, preparing ourselves for a smoother transition.

- If you are running late, communicate! Highly sensitive people tend to be people-pleasers, and we try to push ourselves to be somewhere on time, even if we know it is unlikely. Or, we may get there on time, but we arrive stressed and stretched. A quick call or text when we are running late can reduce our overwhelm and allow us to arrive more present and grounded.

- Pro Tip: Prepare for the unexpected. As much as we would like to be in control of our travel, as the New York City transit system and Los Angeles freeways where I grew up have firmly taught me, travel plans don't always go as expected, even if Google Maps tells us it will only take 47 minutes to get from the San Fernando Valley to LAX airport. (It doesn't.)

## Create a Soothing Routine

Just as a good breakfast sets your day up for success, so can a soothing, calming morning routine. The morning, in particular, can be an overstimulating point of our day, so it is vital to begin it mindfully. It doesn't have to be a complex or time-consuming practice, but something that helps you gently connect with your mind and body and soothe your nervous system before you walk out the door. The moment we open our eyes our brains immediately begin taking in and processing information. As much as we may have been conditioned to believe

the opposite, we do not need to constantly be processing more information than what is happening in front of us, 24/7. It serves a highly
sensitive person better to ease into the barrage of information we get
presented with daily.

Be mindful of what information you consume as you start your day.
With the world at our fingertips via our electronic devices, we may be
tempted to grab our phones and start scrolling right when we wake up.
Consider not checking the news or your social media timelines first, but
begin with another activity that might serve you better. Perhaps you
could journal while sipping on a hot beverage, work out or do yoga, take
a walk, or meditate. Keep it soothing and simple!

Beyond the morning, add "checkpoints" to engage in a mindful and
soothing practice throughout your day. Feel free to write in your own
ideas to give your thinking mind and body a break.

Morning: _____

Afternoon: _____

Evening: Time to wind down! _____

Soothing: _____

## The Art and Practice of Saying No

Highly sensitive people tend to struggle with boundaries, or the beautiful
art of saying no. To avoid overstimulation or unhelpful situations, highly
sensitive people can greatly benefit from becoming more comfortable
refusing or declining requests or suggestions from others. Though it may
at first feel uncomfortable to do so, saying no helps create a boundary
that can benefit us by protecting our time and energy. We only have so
much capacity.

Saying no is also an opportunity to practice some of your sensitive
core skills. "Developing Awareness of Emotions: Naming, Allowing,
and Processing Feelings" (see page 20) will help you discern whether a
no is necessary. If boundary setting is stressful for you, practice "Setting
and Tolerating Boundaries" (see page 23). A few deep breaths while
exhaling will serve your practice.

How to say no in five easy steps:

1. Acknowledge and honor the thing/person/situation you are saying no to.

2. Deliver the message in a firm but kind, tone.

3. Await their response and understand they might feel or express displeasure in your refusal.

4. Tolerate their displeasure or bask in their understanding of your need for a boundary.

5. Carry on!

# TAKEAWAYS

There are many types of highly sensitive people. It is important to identify your type to help yourself better serve your own needs. Recognize that you may be a combination of types though see which you lean toward.

If you discover you are a high sensation–seeking highly sensitive person, play with and discover what balance of stimulation versus downtime feels right.

Managing time and transitions can be a struggle for highly sensitive people. Be kind and compassionate with yourself as you develop this skill.

The art and practice of saying no will empower you to create healthy and helpful boundaries that will serve your highly sensitive nature.

# CHAPTER THREE

# Being a Real Highly Sensitive Person: Social Situations

"What is REAL?" asked Rabbit one day when they were lying side by side near the nursery fender before Nanna came to tidy the room. "Does it mean having things that buzz inside you and a stick-out handle?"

"Real isn't how you are made," said the Skin Horse. "It's a thing that happens to you. When a child loves you for a long, long time, not just to play with, but REALLY loves you, then you become Real."

"Does it hurt?" asked the Rabbit.

"Sometimes," said the Skin Horse, for he was always truthful. "When you are Real you don't mind being hurt."

"Does it happen all at once, like being wound up," he asked, "or bit by bit?"

"It doesn't happen all at once," said the Skin Horse. "You become. It takes a long time. That's why it doesn't happen often to people who break easily or have sharp edges, or who have to be carefully kept. Generally, by the time you are Real, most of your hair has been loved off, and your eyes drop out and you get loose in your joints and very shabby. But these things don't matter at all, because once you are Real you can't be ugly, except to people who don't understand." (Williams 1922)

Presenting our "real" selves can be such a challenge for highly sensitive people. Because we are born into societies, families, and systems that are not always built for our sensitive natures and high emotions and passions, many of us hold back our authentic selves to fit in. A great number of highly sensitive people suffer as a result, though, as all humans do when not allowed to be who they are because of pressures on who they "should" be. Though it can be a struggle, honor your HSP trait. Anything else is betraying your own brain, natural wiring, and psychological need for authenticity.

This chapter discusses expectations of modern society and suggests how to create habits and ways of being to better serve your highly sensitive soul. And, because it is such a huge part of our social lives at this moment, we also look at ways to honor your sensitive trait within the deep and sometimes overwhelming world of social media.

# EXPECTATIONS

In a 2014 fMRI study (Acevedo et al. 2014) done at Stony Brook University, researchers, including HSP pioneer Elaine Aron, discovered that highly sensitive people are wired to have a stronger response to emotional images. The brains of 18 individuals were studied to see how they responded to images of their partners and strangers displaying either positive, negative, or neutral facial expressions. The highly sensitive people of the group had increased brain activation in regions involving empathy, awareness, and sensory processing. They also had more activation in the insula, the part of the brain that helps enhance perception and increases self-awareness.

The mirror neuron system, an area in the brain responsible for empathy and picking up on the emotions of others, saw increased activation and blood flow. This study demonstrates that highly sensitive people have a stronger emotional response to other people's emotions than that of those less sensitive.

This biological difference explains why we as highly sensitive people can have difficulty with social situations and can experience shyness or anxiety. These socially unacceptable traits can also be a symptom of a highly sensitive person learning as they grew up that their emotions and reactions to life situations were wrong. They can be judged by others as "too much" or "too emotional." They need to stop crying, to grow up, be "good." As a result, we can be afraid to show our true selves. Many of my clients also report feeling the need to suppress or withhold their emotions from friends and families. I find this can be especially difficult for highly sensitive men who were wrongly taught "boys don't cry" and that boys and men need to be "tough" to be accepted.

With all of these feelings of judgment, no wonder many of the highly sensitive people I work with report experiencing social anxiety, particularly in large groups, or at parties or other social gatherings. I believe this can be due to a combination of sensory overwhelm and trauma connected to not feeling accepted or "good enough."

Number one among the skills that highly sensitive people must develop to fully embrace themselves is the beautiful gift of crying. Crying is a common topic among the highly sensitive people I work with because they tend to connect more with their tears as they find their authentic natures within the safe and healing space of therapy. I witness many highly sensitive people apologizing the first few times they cry within a session, as though my boxes of tissues are there just for show. When a client expresses shame at their tears, even in a space where they are welcome and allowed to fully express their emotional selves, I hear a sad story of their internalized judgment of crying.

Despite the social message that crying is somehow bad, Dr. William Frey, biochemist and "tear expert," explains quite a different truth. Tears contain stress hormones and other toxins that the body releases through crying. Additionally, other studies show that crying produces endorphins and other "feel good" hormones. There is a biological reason we feel relief after a "good cry."

## On Crying

A simple strategy when tears emerge is simply to allow them to flow, if it feels safe to do so. Be mindful, too, of your thoughts toward yourself when you allow yourself to cry. Sometimes uncomfortable feelings like sadness bring judgmental thoughts. Be sure to practice compassion with yourself as you allow yourself to feel your feelings.

If you must hold back your emotional responses, use your sensitive core skill of "Learning to Soothe" (see page 19) and make a plan for when you would like to cry. Many highly sensitive people prefer to let themselves release when alone and feeling safe. As you begin to practice allowing, containing, or rescheduling your tears, you will begin to find more ease when these beautiful, healing, soothing, human-generated drops flow.

Crying Pro Tip: If you know you might be in a situation where you may cry, or know you have to interact with the public after a good crying session such as after therapy, get yourself some nice crying shades! A good pair of sunglasses can provide a little protection and distance if we are feeling emotional or delicate.

## Working with Social Anxiety

Recognize that it is okay not to love or even like social situations such as large parties, clubs, or crowds. We can acknowledge our natural preferences to have a quieter or less populated life. While you never have to love these big social situations, it is important to learn how to cope and soothe yourself within them if needed.

Embrace silence or "sitting back" if you are feeling uncomfortable or overwhelmed in a social situation. Because many of us are empaths, we can sometimes feel others' discomfort in a situation or feel drawn to "take care" of a group to make everyone else feel more comfortable. This can sometimes lead a highly sensitive person to becoming overwhelmed and emotionally burned out. If we can allow for silence or to sit back, perhaps another part of the group can compensate. Often they will. Self-soothing strategies are generally helpful, even just in the form of a few deep belly breaths, in a situation in which we are experiencing anxiety.

If you want to connect with others, utilize your HSP traits of curiosity and depth. Not surprisingly, many people like and appreciate someone asking questions about them. If you are feeling uncomfortable in a social situation, put on your curiosity cap and ask away. Your amazing mirror neurons might also inspire someone to get more curious about you opening the door for an even deeper connection.

# Rehearse!: A Tool for Social Anxiety

If you are anxious about a particular social event, rehearse how you would like to feel/act/say/leave. Journaling is a great rehearsal venue or simply play out the scene in your mind. Rehearsing for an event in which we feel uncertain can help reduce anxiety.

Several of the sensitive core skills will be helpful as you move through your rehearsal: Practicing "Developing Awareness of Emotions: Naming, Allowing, and Processing Feelings" (see page 20) by noticing and tracking your emotions can help guide you to your needs and wants within the social experience. "Self-advocacy/Self-parenting" (see page 15) and "Setting and Tolerating Boundaries" (see page 23) are also key skills here as you may need to advocate or set boundaries for yourself or others throughout the social event.

Ask yourself the following who, what, where, why, and how questions to help outline and plan for your next social engagement:

**WHO:** Who will be there? Will people be there who know me and understand my sensitive nature? Will I have a sensitive ally present?

**WHAT:** What activity/event will occur? Do I want to participate? Do I have to participate?

**WHERE:** How far do I have to travel? Do I have to drive or can I take public transportation? How much time do I need to reach my destination? How much time will I need to get back home? Bonus: Where can I hide if I need a break?

**WHY:** What is the intention of my presence? Am I going to support someone I care about? Or do I feel obligated to be there?

**HOW:** How would I like to feel before, during, and after the event?

If after going through your rehearsal the event feels like it will be harmful to you or if you find you are experiencing anxiety and overwhelm as you go through your rehearsal questions, this particular event might not be for you. It is okay not to attend. As people-pleasers, highly sensitive people sometimes attend social events that are not ideal or are overwhelming to them. Consider utilizing the "Self-advocacy/Self-parenting" skill (see page 15) and allow yourself to opt out.

# HIGHLY SENSITIVE PEOPLE AND MANAGING SOCIAL SITUATIONS: TREES AND "TRAUMA VOMITS"

I thought the only thing I would need to choose that day was whether to have the beef or salmon at the family friend's wedding I was attending with my husband. After a lovely ceremony, we sat down at table #12 with a group of friendly looking, seemingly harmless strangers. The gentleman next to me began to chat with me and, at first, I happily responded.

Unfortunately, by the time the appetizers were being served, I had not only heard this man's life story but also the death of his mother, cousin, and dog, how his best friend had had a terrible brain cancer diagnosis, and that he had just broken up with his girlfriend.

Though I felt deep compassion for the man, I also felt like I wanted to hide under the table and take a nap. I not only had witnessed his story but without warning or preparation had been the receptacle for his need to process his woes. After the meal was over, he got up from the table to chat with others and hit the dance floor. I sat, exhausted, gazing at my barely touched salmon with a woozy stomach and exhausted heart. I had been the victim of a *trauma vomit*, a term I coined that means being left with the unauthorized emotional yuck of another person. This was not the first time this had happened to me, but at least I had a name for it now.

Trauma vomiting is an unfortunate habit of individuals who tragically have no place to contain their trauma, like a trusted confidant or a healing space or practice. Many humans, when they do not process their trauma, get stuck in telling the story, repeatedly, to any safe person who will listen. They spew their story, which gives them relief, but leaves their listener feeling like taking an emotional or physical shower afterward. Please know that many trauma vomiters are unconscious of what they are doing. They truly are suffering and cannot help but try and find relief wherever they can.

Because other people can sense our nature, highly sensitive people can often be the victim of trauma vomit. This is especially true for those of us who also identify as empaths. You most likely have a friend or family member who trauma vomits on you often and repeatedly. My mother is a master trauma vomiter (sorry, Mom!), but I have used many of the sensitive core skills and other strategies, thus Mom has found alternative places to spew, and I can shower less.

Trauma vomiters also have a well-known cousin, the *psychic* or *energy vampire*. These individuals drain highly sensitive people of vital energy and life force. In my own experience, and that of many of my clients, these energy-sucking souls can be magnetically attracted to our highly sensitive systems.

Many of us highly sensitive people also have difficulty setting boundaries with strangers, when required, because of our enhanced empathy, deep emotional intuition, and propensity toward social anxiety. Many of my clients who live and work in New York City have interactions with strangers on a daily basis. But these interactions create a wonderful opportunity to practice the skills of "Self-advocacy/Self-parenting" (see page 15) and "Setting and Tolerating Boundaries" (see page 23).

Example: A stranger approaches and asks for your phone number. You immediately notice your discomfort and impulse to get away, advocate for yourself by saying "no, thank you," and set a boundary by removing yourself from the situation.

All humans, but especially highly sensitive people, can be deeply affected by emotionally fraught stories and images, including those on our social media feeds. A scroll down our timelines can suddenly thrust us into someone else's trauma. Of course, we can also experience happiness and joy from social media posts, but even a seemingly harmless or fun account we might be following can suddenly take a turn.

For example, Enrique, a client of mine, had been following the Internet account of a person who illustrated positive messages with a special-needs cat. Wonderful, right? Unfortunately, the cat passed away from health complications. Upon opening his Instagram account, Enrique became grief-stricken and fell into mourning. As the days passed, Enrique continued reading the owner's grieving posts. Enrique expressed empathy and shed a few tears.

As the weeks went on, the owner continued posting about his grief. Enrique surprised himself by finally reaching a point where he felt angry reading the mournful posts. He sat with his anger and realized he had had enough. The full extent of this grief was not his. He had needed to recognize this, especially because he had reached his emotional saturation point. Though he at first felt guilty for doing so, he listened to his feelings and unfollowed.

If you find yourself in Enrique's position, where you are noticing and observing your emotional responses and practicing your skill of "Developing Awareness of Overstimulation" (see page 16), you might want to consider additional sensitive core skills to incorporate.

Our relationships to social media can provide a perfect opportunity to practice these sensitive core skills, as Enrique's experience demonstrates. With the skills "Developing Awareness of Overstimulation" (see page 16) and "Developing Awareness of Emotions: Naming, Allowing, and Processing Feelings" (see page 20), Enrique was able to be more cognizant of his emotional landscape. "Setting and Tolerating Boundaries" (see page 23) helped him assess what he needed and take action toward that. What sensitive core skills might enable you to restructure your relationship with social media?

## Self-Care in Social Situations

A highly sensitive person must practice the following self-care strategies to help promote their overall well-being in social situations.

- Take breaks when you need to! Highly sensitive people can feel pressure to be "on" in social situations far longer than they generally prefer. If you begin to notice yourself getting exhausted or drained in a social situation such as at a party, please allow yourself a break for as much time as you need. You can sit quietly in another room, take a walk outside, or find a furry, nonverbal companion to socialize with.

- Respect your body's signals in terms of what you are consuming and for how long you participate in the social situation. We can sometimes ignore the cues our minds and bodies provide that let us know we have reached our limit. Or we might consume something we otherwise would not. Embrace the notion of leaving without telling anyone, or practice the skill of setting a boundary ("no, thank you," to that next drink) if you need to.

- If you encounter a social situation with a difficult person, a difficult energy (I'm sure you know what I mean), read the next section with a tool to help from my friend, Ram Dass.

## Managing and Accepting Difficult People: Turning People into Trees

Spiritual teacher Ram Dass beautifully illustrated how human beings place limitations on one another and ultimately on themselves when they do not allow their natural states to just be, much as nature just is. Ram Dass spoke in his teachings about the struggle human beings experience when they have difficulty accepting people for who they are. Somehow, we can easily accept nature, such as trees, no matter their kind, size, or which way they are growing, while we struggle to accept other humans the same way.

To help us along in accepting others, we can practice turning people, especially difficult ones, into trees—beings we fully accept, whatever type of tree they might be, whatever direction they are growing, accepting them exactly as they are. This can also be an opportunity to utilize your innate skills of "Reframing Difficult Situations" (see page 24) to create more comfort. Additionally, this presents a wonderful opportunity to practice "Setting and Tolerating Boundaries" (see page 23), if needed.

In action, this can look like accepting the aggravating co-worker or relative by accepting who they are rather than trying to change them. A phrase often used in the practice of therapy is "meet people where they are"; in other words, accept and acknowledge where an individual is in their emotional development and work from there.

So, if you have a family member with the emotional intelligence of a toddler (yes, these humans exist!), it would be unhelpful to both of you if you expected them to be an emotional adult. If they act like a three-year-old, then hold your expectations of them to that standard. See if you can "meet this person where they are" while advocating for your own needs. The core skills of "Self-advocacy/Self-parenting" (see page 15) and "Honoring and Responding to Truth and Justice" (see page 21) are important here, and you may need to practice "Setting and Tolerating Boundaries" (see page 23).

# Managing Stranger Danger

Interacting with strangers is an opportunity to practice advocating for yourself, as well as holding boundaries in a low-stakes way. Many of my clients first practice "Setting and Tolerating Boundaries" (see page 23) and "Self-advocacy/Self-parenting" (see page 15) with strangers to strengthen their skill set. If you don't get the results you'd like, you probably won't see this person again anyway, so it's a safe way to practice. You might choose public transportation venues such as buses and trains, or large public spaces such as malls, supermarkets, and parks.

**STEP 1:** Using your HSP trait of intuition and attunement, take a quick assessment of the stranger you are going to interact with. Do they seem safe and approachable? If yes, proceed to step 2.

**STEP 2:** Communicate what you would like to say. This can be a request such as, "Pardon me sir/madam/fellow human, could I sit in the empty seat next to you?" Or, sometimes simply complimenting someone can be an easy way to practice interacting with strangers.

**STEP 3:** Actively listen and adjust to their response. They may have a simple "thank you" if you go the compliment route, or they might shift to let you sit in that empty seat.

**STEP 4:** If you feel the interaction is not going well, begin to feel unsafe, or find you have encountered a trauma vomiter or psychic or energy vampire, you can make your graceful exit. Using your sensitive core skill of "Setting and Tolerating Boundaries" (see page 23), and your innate trait of excellent communication, politely excuse yourself and leave the situation.

**STEP 4A (OPTIONAL):** At this point, you might be a little more attuned to the person you are speaking with, so if you'd like, spark up a conversation with them. It does not have to be anything special or extraordinary, just a moment-to-moment human connection.

**STEP 5:** After the interaction is complete, review either in writing or within your own mind how the interaction felt. Do you feel fulfilled by the interaction? Were there any surprises? Did you enjoy it? What would you do differently next time?

Tips for Managing Stranger Danger:

- Employ an emotional bodyguard. My husband, after the dreaded wedding trauma vomit episode, has been employed as my permanent emotional bodyguard. We now have an explicit agreement that if I give him a certain signal, he will graciously assist me in moving away from or creating a boundary with trauma vomiters or psychic or energy vampires.

- Always trust your intuition if a stranger feels unsafe or dangerous. Highly sensitive people are excellent at perceiving and intuiting other people. If your gut tells you not to interact with someone, listen to yourself and don't do it. You aren't crazy or unkind, you might just be picking up something from another person that others do not see.

- Strangers are people, too. Though it is important to first trust our gut instincts and remove ourselves from dangerous people and situations, generally, most strangers are not out to harm us.

## De-Stressing Your Social Media Timeline

Recognize we are currently living in a time of TMI (too much information), especially online. You are not required to witness others' lives constantly, especially if you don't personally know them. You are entitled and allowed to take breaks from social media or not have any accounts at all. Remember that getting on social media is neither your job nor necessary. One can exist without a Facebook or Instagram account and still lead a healthy and fulfilled life.

If you do choose to be online, curate your feed to one that feels emotionally healthy and fulfilling. Many of my HSP clients report they prefer Instagram to Facebook because they can just choose visual images they find pleasing or joyful without the written, emotional impact that Facebook can sometimes provide. Don't wait until you have reached your social media breaking point before leaving your feed; instead, proactively evaluate your relationship to social media and who and what you are following. Because of the pace and structure of social media, we might be unconsciously consuming too much information that may be unhelpful or harmful in the long run.

When you are online, be mindful of your feeling state, and pay attention to when your system might be signaling to you that you need to create a boundary or unfollow certain accounts, like our friend Enrique from earlier in the chapter. Many social media platforms have tools, such as the "unfollow" feature on Facebook or "mute" on Instagram, to maintain connection to someone's account without having to witness their daily posts.

# TAKEAWAYS

Our sensitivity to the world and social situations is not because we are weak or ill-suited for the outside world; it's because we are truly biologically wired this way. Develop compassion for your unique brain chemistry and learn to work with it through your newly acquired HSP skills and strategies.

Though it is incredibly human to project certain thoughts and feelings onto people we do not know, I generally find that many people can be kind, compassionate, and generous. I see examples of this every single day in New York City. Don't forget: 20 percent of the population is also highly sensitive!

Managing how we interact with others in social situations creates wonderful opportunities to practice skills such as "Self-advocacy/Self-parenting" (see page 15) and "Setting and Tolerating Boundaries" (see page 23), as well as strengthening and honoring our innate HSP skills.

# CHAPTER FOUR

# Open Heart Living: Relationships

Zen Master Thich Nhat Hanh wrote "To love is to recognize, to be loved is to be recognized by the other." Love and matters of the heart, whether romantic, family, or friend are central to a highly sensitive person's well-being. Though we may need more alone time to rest and recharge from human interactions, we also require and crave deep, authentic, and meaningful connections in all our intimate relationships. We highly sensitive people lead with our hearts, attune to the ones we love, and offer empathy. All of this connection sometimes tires us out. As highly sensitive people, we love deeply, but because of our big and sensitive souls, we can be hurt deeply as well. In this chapter, we will discuss how to work with your innate sensitivity within your intimate relationships while striving toward helping your loved ones recognize and honor your sensitive trait.

# COMMON CHALLENGES FOR AND RESEARCH ON HIGHLY SENSITIVE PEOPLE IN ROMANTIC RELATIONSHIPS

Though highly sensitive people are known to be wonderful, caring, compassionate, and empathetic partners, they can encounter difficulties in their romantic relationships in terms of honoring, managing, and communicating about their HSP trait. We will first explore some of the current research regarding highly sensitive people in romantic relationships, then turn to strategies to help highly sensitive people have happier and healthier relationships.

Elaine Aron found in a 2004 study that highly sensitive people tend to get bored more easily in romantic relationships than those who are less sensitive. This may be due in part to an intensive need for deep emotional processing and a partner's inability to fulfill it. However, if we happen to choose a mate who is also highly sensitive, they can share our processing needs.

Aron also found that highly sensitive people, especially high sensation–seeking highly sensitive people, tend to enjoy sex more and be more open to different types of social and gender constructs and experiences than their less sensitive partners. Though this has yet to be studied, I hypothesize that many individuals who identify with broader gender expectations and sexual orientations are likely to be highly sensitive. These individuals allow themselves to play and explore in the spectrums of gender and sexuality without necessarily being withheld by cultural constructs.

Highly sensitive people tend to have an almost spiritual connection to sex. Many of us can enjoy the mystery and power of our own sexuality and because of our sensitive nervous systems can also experience sexual pleasure with more subtle stimuli. A brief touch or longing glance can be electrifying to a highly sensitive person. I wonder if individuals who practice healing through intimate and sexual means, such as professional cuddlers or sexual surrogates, tend toward highly sensitive as well.

That highly sensitive people are far more likely to be affected by others' moods and have a stronger response to others' emotions can mean having a hypervigilance to our loved one's facial expressions and mood states. This hypervigilance tends to be particularly prevalent if the highly sensitive person suffered childhood trauma, especially attachment trauma. Our deep attunement can sometimes be confusing for highly sensitive people. At those times when we sense anger or annoyance from our partner, misunderstandings can arise and the highly sensitive person can feel defensive. We may believe their mood is due to us even when it is not. It is vital that highly sensitive people practice healthy communication in their romantic relationships to avoid such confusion or misunderstandings.

Some highly sensitive people struggle with getting their central needs met because prior experiences and relationships have convinced them that they are undeserving. We are not special or "needy" when making requests about how we should be treated within a relationship, even if others who misunderstand or judge our HSP trait try to make us feel that way. Asking for what we want and need should be central to any relationship.

## Reframe Relationship Expectations

Despite what Hallmark and Lifetime movies say, your partner does not have to be your everything. Because both highly sensitive people and those less sensitive have come to expect the be-all partner, we sometimes experience disappointment in intimate relationships when our partners do not fulfill our every emotional, spiritual, and social need, or does not like the same activities or things that we do. In her 2007 book, *Mating in Captivity,* relationship and infidelity expert Esther Perel hypothesizes that many modern relationships fail because we put too much pressure on our partners to be our best friends, lovers, and everything in between (2007). Through her research, she discovered that individuals who have more social resources tend to be happier in their intimate and long-term relationships.

Your partner is, of course, one of the most important relationships of your life, but you may want to explore the possibility that you can be fulfilled in certain categories by other important relationships. For example, if you have a desire to see live theater and your partner hates it, invite some theater-loving friends along instead, or join a group of theater goers instead of dragging your partner.

View your romantic relationships as not only a relational component of your life but as a spiritual and healing opportunity. Just as we can be traumatized and wounded within relationships, we can also utilize our relationships as vehicles for healing. Studies of couples and family systems have shown that human beings often unconsciously choose a partner who replicates their first experiences of love, reflecting the ways in which we first learned about love through our families and close relationships growing up.

Because we are led by this familiar feeling we know as "love," we might find ourselves in relational difficulties and situations similar to the ones we witnessed in our parents or caregivers growing up. For example, if an individual grows up with a parent who struggled with an addiction, this person is far more likely to unconsciously choose someone with a similar difficulty. Though it can be stressful to make this discovery, this relational mirroring can also be a wonderful opportunity to consciously work through these difficulties and perhaps break a cycle of hurt and pain that has existed within a family for generations.

Though it may seem a bit daunting, this might also be the perfect opportunity for you to practice some of your sensitive core skills. For example, if you came from a family where boundaries were not clear or acceptable, you and your partner can create some. It can look as simple as consciously assigning different household duties to each other. Or if your family was not accepting of emotions, perhaps you and your partner work to ensure all emotions are allowed into your interactions with each other, as uncomfortable as they may feel.

Despite the fact that romantic relationships can be a beautiful tool for conscious spiritual growth and healing, be cautious in trying to "fix" your partner. Be clear on whether staying in a romantic relationship with similar issues to those you experienced in your family of origin is indeed safe and healing for you or if the "fixing" and "healing" is another interpretation of past family dysfunction.

Allow yourself to be unconfined by the rigid rules of romantic relationships or constructs. I assume that highly sensitive people are more likely to get bored within relationships because many of us tend toward boredom or frustration with all culturally acceptable constructs, including romantic relationships and gender expectations. Don't limit yourself to classic gender and relationship roles if they do not feel authentic to you.

# Create Healthy Communication and Boundaries

Your partner may not intuitively know how to understand your emotional needs. We sometimes carry the belief that because our partner is with us and loves us they can intuit our needs and know what we want. If our partner is not highly sensitive, we may carry the unconscious perception they see and experience the world the way we do. Though it would make it easier to communicate if our partner were a mind reader, our relationships will be more beneficial if we find methods of healthy communication and boundary setting.

- Educate your partner about the HSP trait. Thankfully, there are now many wonderful resources such as books, articles, Ted Talks, and the films *Sensitive: The Untold Story* and *Sensitive and in Love* that you could share with your partner. Read or watch these resources together. Speak with your partner about what aspects of these resources you identify with. This can also be an opportunity for your partner to discuss any of the challenges they encounter in your relationship if they are not highly sensitive.

- Before discussing your highly sensitive trait with your partner, define for yourself your relationship anxiety, anger, and fight triggers. These triggers might be displays of anger, fear of abandonment, or loss of individuality. Consider how your unique, highly sensitive nature might come into play.

- Learn conscious communication techniques through self-education, or through seeing a qualified couples' counselor or marriage and family therapist. As highly sensitive people, most of us prefer authenticity and clear communication in our relationships.

- If you have ever been in an abusive romantic relationship, identify and discuss issues you may be unconsciously bringing to your current relationship or might need to further process. This is also something that would benefit from working with a therapist.

- Learn your attachment style. All humans bring their own attachment style to their relationships: secure, anxious, avoidant or, for most, a mixture of all three. In their 2011 book, *Attached*, authors Levine and

Heller explain the science behind attachment styles and how to work with them in romantic relationships. Learning about you and your partner's attachment styles can serve your relationship greatly, as it can reveal some of the unconscious patterns or difficulties you may face in your relationship. It might explain why sometimes your partner feels "clingy" (anxious attachment) or why you might sometimes put off intimacy (avoidant).

• Consciously, clearly, and calmly discuss with your partner what physical, emotional and sexual boundaries you might need in the relationship and ways you'd like to communicate. If you are unsure, take time to explore these boundaries within yourself before speaking with your partner about them. If you are in individual therapy, it would greatly serve you to bring this up with your therapist. See if you can find a way to work and compromise with these needs compassionately and respectfully. Seek relationship counseling if you need guidance or support.

## To Swipe or Not to Swipe? Highly Sensitive People and Dating

Dating apps and websites are currently the most popular method of finding a mate. Though some of my HSP clients love dating apps because they eliminate the anxiety around approaching a potential partner on the spot, others report frustration because they can't utilize their deeper instincts and intuitions through technology. If you can relate to these frustrations, take assurance! People are still also meeting in the "old fashioned," in-person way when out with friends or through mutual friends, for example.

When we do find a person to date, highly sensitive people can get caught up in new relationship energy (NRE). This rush of romantic excitement can temporarily blind our sensitive eyes to possible red flags or issues that might emerge with a new partner as the relationship deepens. Though there is nothing necessarily wrong with a relationship moving at a rapid pace, be cautious about getting caught up in the momentum and excitement of a new relationship.

Trust your gut and instincts about a person whom you may date, especially if you are aware you might be experiencing NRE. Take some time to sit with what is beyond your infatuation and excitement with this person. It can also be helpful to process your excitement with a friend or therapist.

If it feels safe, speak with the person or person(s) you are dating about your highly sensitive nature. They might be highly sensitive, too! It also gives you an opportunity to practice speaking about and educating another person about it. If after a little while of being together discussing your HSP trait doesn't feel safe, this may be a sign they're not the right partner or partners for you.

Compassionately manage your expectations about your dating life. We tend to put a lot of pressure on ourselves in the dating process and can be self-judgmental if things don't work out the way we imagined. Yes, dating functions as a search for a partner, but it can also be a process of discovering what we want in a relationship and practice being in one. Though unsuccessful dates can often feel and be framed as a disappointment or failure, they are also an opportunity to teach us our needs and wants in our romantic relationships.

# SENSITIVE FAMILY MATTERS

"Are you sleeping?"

After a long cross-country flight from New York to California, I am finally in the place I had been dreaming about for months: on my parent's living room couch, wrapped tightly in a fuzzy blanket as I nap, my dog snuggled at my feet. Apparently, my dear and unintentionally annoying father was confused about whether I was napping. Perhaps my closed eyes and blanket burrito status left the question open.

"Yes," I croak, peeling one of my tired eyes open to address him. I pull the blanket over my head as I hear my younger brother enter the room.

"Napping again? Why are you so tired?" At this point, I realize I will no longer get any rest in this public space, scoop up my blanket and dog, and find quiet and respite in my childhood bedroom.

Explaining and defending my need for delicious couch naps is a common struggle for me and many other highly sensitive people. This is not just about the naps. Many highly sensitive people can find it difficult to explain their needs and create healthy boundaries with family and romantic partners.

Furthermore, as many highly sensitive people begin their own families, they struggle with the high demands of parenting, balancing their adult relationships with raising children, while also possibly managing the needs of elderly parents.

## Black Sheep Energy

Feeling like we do not belong to the group we were born into can be devastating and isolating. The majority of brave human beings who enter my office to begin their healing work speak of feeling weird, odd, or left out of their families. They need, love, and desire different aspects of the world. Their priorities and value systems don't match what they were taught growing up. They often feel wrong and different, like the black sheep of their families. My own personal and clinical work has taught me how harmful denying one's authentic self can be. On the flip side, there is immense freedom and joy when we do allow ourselves to be exactly who we are, even if that makes us different from the rest of the flock. So, my proposition to you is, rather than hide your gorgeous illustrious wool under a disguise of non-sensitive, suppressive clothing, own and—if you'd like—flaunt exactly how you are.

Black sheep energy is a *mindset*, in which we own, fully, that we are different from the flock and are proud of it! We acknowledge gracefully that our needs, wants, desires, and values are different from those of our family, and we don't feel the need to apologize for it. This mindset allows us the confidence to be our amazing selves. This can look like making our own life choices, such as where we live, who we love, and what political affiliations and social causes we might align with.

If you do resonate with your black sheep status, contemplate ways in which you can practice being with and honoring your black sheep self! How can you allow yourself to live and be more authentic to your true nature? Perhaps you have been afraid to tell your parents your political views. See if you might want to share them! Or maybe you have a family member who has difficulty holding healthy boundaries with you. See if you can begin to lay a few down. Or you have been wanting to start a creative project or venture but have been afraid you'd be mocked or ridiculed if you did. Brush your wool off and pick up that paintbrush or pen if you like. Your life is your choice. You don't have to be like the rest of the flock.

Black sheep have been around since the beginning of humanity, and thank goodness for that. Scholars, artists, activists, and anyone who has dared to break the societal mold have all been black sheep. Without them, and without you, think how boring and confining life could be. By owning your authentic self, you are not only helping heal yourself but the world at large. Authenticity can be contagious. So, fluff up your gorgeous wool, polish those hooves, and *baa baa*, my friend. *Baa baa!*

## Holiday Survival Guide

Just as those dubious Hallmark and Lifetime movies and shiny social media posts model unrealistic romantic expectations, they also tell us that extended time with family, especially during the holidays, is filled with joy, fun, and togetherness. Many highly sensitive people, however, find the holidays physically and emotionally draining. Here are some strategies to make your holidays more HSP friendly and more enjoyable.

- Create a mindful enter-and-exit strategy. Before you speak with family about travel arrangements or book any transportation tickets, consider your own needs FIRST. Outline the amount of time you would like to visit family. On average, most enjoy about three to four days with family before needing a break of a day or two or to leave entirely.

- Establish an emergency plan. If you come from a difficult or dysfunctional family, still want to have the holiday with them, but find spending time with them distressing, have an emergency plan in case any situation becomes too volatile. This plan can look like leaving early or having a friend, hotel, or place of respite nearby if you need a break. Even something simple like taking a walk around the neighborhood to recover from a difficult interaction can be helpful.

- Make self-care a priority. Utilize your black sheep energy to support your needs for naps, breaks, or downtime. No need to apologize for it. It is just what a black sheep needs.

- Create extra lines of communication or a method to process any feelings that may arise (or both) that are separate from your family, if you need support. Ask your therapist, a friend, or co-worker if they could be there just in case. Journaling can also be an accessible and quiet way to process your feelings.

- Be on the lookout for fellow familial black sheep! Because high sensitivity is genetic, others in your family system may be highly sensitive yet don't realize it. This person may be your ally in difficult situations.

- Don't leave your baggage unattended. Just as you need to keep a close watch on your bags as you move through an airplane terminal, be aware of the emotional baggage you might be bringing to family holidays or the baggage that might get consciously or unconsciously unpacked by your family members while you are visiting. Before the visit, review emotional issues of the past and present that may arise, and think through how you would like to react.

- The holidays also present opportunities to practice some of your core sensitive skills. The skills of "Self-advocacy/Self-parenting" (see page 15) and "Setting and Tolerating Boundaries" (see page 23) work beautifully together as you plan a family holiday experience that works best for you. You can also practice "Reframing Difficult Situations" (see page 24) since being with family can be difficult. This can also pair with the skill of "Honoring and Developing Joy and Creativity" (see page 22). Perhaps you can use your creative skills to create a new family ritual that everyone, including you, can enjoy.

## On Parenting and for Parents

Societal norms help drive cultural and familial pressures to have children. If you are unsure if you want children, you are entitled to take your time and decide consciously, on your own or with your partner, whether to have children at all.

Creating and caring for another human being is a 24/7, extremely taxing job, especially for highly sensitive people. You do not have to have a child if you do not want to. But if you still have the desire to care for someone else, consider if this need has to be accomplished via the standard methods. We can parent those around us, our pets, other children we have in our lives, or the planet. Or you can just parent yourself!

If you do want children or already have them, please know that many highly sensitive people make excellent parents but find it stressful because it is neverending. Elaine Aron has found that highly sensitive parents' homes can be more disorganized or chaotic than those of less sensitive parents (2015). However, she also found that highly sensitive people show more attunement with the children in the household than their less sensitive counterparts. I am privileged to work with some highly sensitive parents and am awed by their deep love, empathy, and connection to their children. These parents strive to be conscious of their children's emotional experiences and deeply want to give these children the well-nurtured childhood they themselves did not have.

Recognize that because of the HSP propensity to be overwhelmed, highly sensitive parents must have compassion for themselves and ask for assistance when needed. Doing so models vulnerability for the children and that it is okay to ask for help.

I also view parenting as an amazing opportunity for restorative experiences surrounding how we ourselves were parented. Though we cannot change our childhoods, we can, within limits, give our child an entirely different childhood experience. We did not have a choice in how our sensitivity or emotional development was handled, but if we decide to parent consciously, we can raise our children to have the space and freedom to be their authentic selves. We can allow our children to have healthy boundaries, express their emotions freely, teach them to self-regulate, allow them to tell the truth of who they are, and enable them to play fully and develop their own innate creativity.

Because HSP traits are innate and inborn, it might be likely that your children are highly sensitive as well. There are many wonderful resources for HSP children such as *The Highly Sensitive Child* by Elaine Aron or *The Strong, Sensitive Boy* by Ted Zeff. For more, see the Resources section at the end of this book (page 111).

If you do feel parenting is your calling but are overwhelmed by the thought of it, please take heed, my dear highly sensitive person. We are absolutely capable and up to the task. Please do not let your sensitivity get in the way of creating the family you desire.

# HIGHLY SENSITIVE FRIENDSHIPS

Highly sensitive people make wonderful friends. We are conscientious, caring, loyal, empathetic, and excellent listeners. We deeply value our friendships because we get to choose them.

Many highly sensitive people, though, also find friendships challenging because many of us have difficulty acknowledging and honoring our needs and communicating them to our friends. We might also feel social pressure to conform or suppress our own individual needs to try to be like "everyone else." We might have a different set of social needs and preferences from our less sensitive friends. Also, having difficult conversations, such as confronting a friend over an issue, can be difficult for highly sensitive people in that they can be overwhelming and anxiety-provoking.

You will develop a deeper awareness and consciousness of your friendships as you learn about and honor your highly sensitive nature. In the following sections, you will learn ways to manage your current friendships and certain issues that may arise with friends who are not highly sensitive. You will also learn strategies for establishing your own HSP community.

## Conscious Friendships

Like with all relationships, occasionally taking stock of our friendships can be beneficial. One way to do this is to develop a deeper consciousness around our friendships, especially those we might find difficult or challenging.

The checklist on page 67 can help you explore your current friendships. Know that just as with romantic partners, we sometimes unconsciously choose friends that mirror our familial relationships because they feel "familiar." It is that comforting feeling when you first meet someone but feel you have known them all your life.

This familiarity, of course, is not always a sign that a relationship is unhealthy. But especially if your family system includes dysfunctional dynamics, evaluating your friendships more deeply can be a benefit to your highly sensitive self. If your intuition signals that something feels off, pay attention. A re-evaluation does not automatically mean a friendship might need to end, but it can indicate a need for boundaries or a shift in roles or communication patterns. If you find that a friendship is no longer serving you or feels toxic, consider pausing or ending the friendship.

1. Do you sometimes feel misunderstood or not as cared for as you might like?

2. Is there an emotional imbalance? Do you feel you are constantly caretaking, parenting, or "therapizing" your friends?

3. When you spend time with this person, do you feel like you are always talking about their issues and don't spend time on your problems as well? Is this dynamic comfortable for you?

4. Does it feel safe to communicate an issue or a problem you might be having?

5. Is there a possibility your friend could be a "trauma vomiter" or "psychic or energy vampire"?

6. Do you tend to hold back your authentic feelings toward a friend in fear of upsetting them?

7. Do you ever feel like you have to "walk on eggshells" with some of your friends?

8. Do any of your friendships remind you of relationships you have with siblings or any other close family members? If yes, who and how?

9. Do you feel your friend understands and honors your highly sensitive nature? Does this person understand and make adjustments to a situation that might feel overwhelming to you, such as not enjoying crowded bars or restaurants?

10. Do you ever feel you have outgrown a friendship but maintain it out of guilt or history with the person?

11. Is your friendship "flexible"? As your circumstances change (e.g., going to college, getting married, or growing emotionally), can your friendship "tolerate" these changes? This can look like understanding and honoring new boundaries, roles, and ways of communicating.

12. How do you feel when you are with this person? How does your body feel when you are interacting? Are you relaxed, tense, or somewhere in between?

13. How do you feel before spending time with them? Are you full of excitement or dread?

14. Do you ever engage in activities or consumption with your friend(s) in ways you feel do not serve you in your current life, but you continue to engage anyway? This might look like staying out late, drinking heavily, or using drugs.

15. After spending time with this person, how do your mind and body feel? Are you fulfilled or depleted?

If your answers to this quiz give you concern about your friendship, this could be a sign that a friendship needs to be re-evaluated or the roles and boundaries of it might need to shift. This means you may have to have a difficult conversation with this person. Here are some tips and strategies for having that difficult conversation.

## Gentle Confrontations: Having Difficult Conversations with Friends

Evaluate the person you want to confront. Utilizing your HSP nature of deep intuition and attunement, think about if this person will be open and willing to do what you need. Do they currently have the capability of making the changes you are asking for? This is not about judging the other person or holding them to unrealistic emotional expectations, but it is about meeting them where they are emotionally. If you feel they might be unwilling or incapable of making the changes you are requesting, consider turning them into a tree (see "Self-advocacy/Self-parenting," page 15, or "Setting or Tolerating Boundaries," page 23).

I find in-person confrontations most effective, but they might be overwhelming for some highly sensitive people. If you feel it is unbearable to discuss your issues with your friend in person, send them a letter or email explaining your issues. A phone call can be less overwhelming as well. You might want to tell them why you are choosing to confront in this fashion rather than in person. Hopefully, knowing your highly sensitive nature, your friend will be understanding about your method of confrontation.

If you do decide to speak about your issues in person, consider the time and place for approaching them. Confrontation can be very uncomfortable for many highly sensitive people, as it can for all humans, especially if we do not have a lot of practice with it. To ease this discomfort, find a time and place that ideally will be less stimulating or anxiety-provoking. A private or quiet space, where you and your friend can express yourselves freely and with fewer restrictions on time.

You will likely feel some anxiety and overwhelm before, during, and after your confrontation, so please practice your "Learning to Soothe: Working with Our 'Self-Cleaning Oven'" skill (see page 19) when needed. Take deep breaths and ground when you need to. It can also be helpful to wear comfortable clothes or bring a small comfort item with you, such as a soft scarf or cozy hoodie.

Rehearse! It can be helpful to write down what you would like to say first, perhaps as a letter to your friend. Do a free write, meaning write what you want to say without carefully crafting your words or attempting to take care of their needs so as to not upset the other person. This can enable you to clearly acknowledge in a low-stakes way what you want. After your first draft, refine your words in the way you find most effective.

Utilize your black sheep energy (see page 62) to empower you to advocate for yourself. Because of past experiences of not getting your emotional needs met, or possibly not even knowing you have the right to have them met, the idea of confronting another person and, shockingly, being heard might feel foreign and "wrong" somehow. It is not! Honoring your authentic nature serves both you and your friendship.

Before you begin with your main message, be clear about what your intention is for the confrontation with yourself and with your friend. If you are uncomfortable, scared, or nervous about the confrontation, name your feelings. Continue to name your feelings throughout the conversation if doing so helps relieve tension or stress.

Example: I am very nervous to speak with you about this, but because I care deeply about you and value our friendship, I felt it was better if I said this to you. . . .

Know that your friend might not initially react the way you would like. They may, in fact, get defensive or angry with you. Hold, honor, and reflect their feelings as best you can, while still acknowledging you have the right to your own feelings. If the conversation begins to feel toxic, blaming, shaming, or unproductive, take a break and revisit the issue later.

It is okay to acknowledge that some friendships are not meant to last forever! Human beings are constantly changing, shifting, and growing. Though highly sensitive people typically prefer more deep and meaningful relationships, friendships can come to a natural end.

## Finding HSP Friends and Community

Having friends and an HSP community can be a tremendous gift to our highly sensitive selves. This is true for highly sensitive people who are also introverts. Creating these social connections can help normalize our experiences and provide the quality and depth of relationships we desire.

Despite many of their inherent flaws, Facebook groups can be an accessible and less overwhelming way of finding and connecting with fellow highly sensitive people. I can attest to this personally. I found the "Highly Sensitive Therapists" Facebook group where I am able to talk with highly sensitive therapists, like me, from all kinds of places. I love that I can seek support through this group. Usually within a few minutes of posting, I receive wonderful, loving feedback.

If social media is not your thing, search for possible HSP meetups in your area through websites such as Meetup.com. You may also find other highly sensitive people at activities we tend to enjoy, such as art classes, concerts, or book clubs. Consider volunteering at places that might also interest other highly sensitive people such as an animal shelter, food pantry, or community garden. You can help others and possibly make meaningful contacts.

Because of the work of Elaine Aron and many other highly sensitive researchers, pioneers, and teachers, the world is finally becoming more familiar with high sensitivity and the value of its traits. There may very likely be a training, presentation, or retreat in your area where you could meet fellow highly sensitive people. Or consider traveling to an HSP event in which you have an interest.

## TAKEAWAYS

Authenticity, respectful communication, and healthy boundaries are vital in a highly sensitive person's relationships. Enacting these skills can feel uncomfortable and daunting, but with patience and practice, they can help strengthen and deepen your most important and intimate relationships.

Though I discussed the skill of gentle confrontations (see page 68) in terms of friendships that need adjustment, know that you can use this communication technique with your romantic or familial relationships as well.

Despite the status, length, or circumstances of a relationship, if it feels toxic or abusive, you always, always have the right to end a relationship, even with family members. Sometimes there is nothing we can do to change a relationship, despite our efforts, and it can be best to love someone from a distance.

If you are finding great difficulty or are experiencing a high level of anxiety or overwhelm at the thought of asking that your intimate needs be met or boundaries be set, or in ending a toxic or abusive relationship, look for a deeper or subconscious reason for your internal resistance. If you are in therapy, this would be a very helpful topic to discuss with your therapist. If you are not, consider seeking therapy if you feel distressed in your intimate relationships.

# CHAPTER FIVE

# Finding Flow: Highly Sensitive People in Work and Vocation

Highly sensitive people can find identifying a job, career, vocation, or even a calling to be a challenge. Because of the needs of our finely tuned nervous systems, we tend to seek more meaning in our work and can struggle with work-life balance.

First, some clarification on what I mean when I say *job, career, vocation,* and *calling.* I see a job as what someone does to pay the bills and make ends meet but not necessarily something they devote soul energy to. So, someone may have a job at a company and view it as a temporary, pragmatic stop on their way to a more permanent position in which they are more emotionally invested (i.e., a career). I see vocation as a more practical skill that someone engages in because they love it or have a genuine interest. For whatever reason, though, a person's vocation may not be how they make money. So, a lawyer whose career is in finance on Wall Street may have a vocation as an English teacher for ESL students. A calling could be a career or a vocation but is what someone's driven to do from a place of passion or purpose. Someone can be "called," for example, to be a doctor, missionary, or actor but not everyone can identify their true calling.

Aligning the needs of the highly sensitive person with the demands, pace, and environmental factors of the modern workplace can create some unique challenges, both in choosing a job, career, or vocation, and in making day-to-day work life manageable, sustainable, and meaningful.

This chapter presents strategies related to choosing a job, career, or vocation that suits the needs of a highly sensitive person as well as strategies for managing aspects of the workplace. I also share experiences of real highly sensitive people who have found effective ways to create the work-life combination they desire.

# IDENTIFYING YOUR INTERESTS: JOBS, CAREERS, AND VOCATIONS FOR HIGHLY SENSITIVE PEOPLE

Highly sensitive people can struggle with identifying their calling or having a clear vision of the job, career, or vocation that might be best suited for them. Because they are often encouraged to ignore their sensitive natures and instincts, this repression can also, unfortunately, show up in how they create and build their working life.

"What do you want to be when you grow up?" The million-dollar question of childhood. Highly sensitive people lucky enough to have grown up in a supportive and safe environment may have been encouraged to explore their interests and figure out where their talents and greatest abilities lay. But supportive home or not, some of us were discouraged, rejected, or otherwise taught to repress our calling and authentic interests. Perhaps you can resonate with the deep frustration of having a sense or intuition of what you were interested in or wanted to study and feeling familial or societal pressure to choose a job or career that did not suit your authentic nature.

A 2019 study by Esther Bergsma surveyed over 5,500 highly sensitive people in 10 countries and found that those from places with better economic standing and more opportunities had the advantage of being able to pick a more meaningful and HSP-suited career. Though highly sensitive people from less prosperous countries still possessed a desire for more meaningful work, economic safety and possible career opportunities won out. These findings highlight the sometimes-difficult economic choices some highly sensitive people must make when choosing their work.

Many highly sensitive people report finding great joy in work that involves creativity such as being a writer, musician, artist, or graphic designer; or in such helping careers as psychotherapist, massage therapist, nurse, or teacher. Many of the positions highly sensitive people enjoy the most lend themselves to the experience known as *flow*. Researcher Mihaly Csikszentmihalyi first published a book in 1990 on flow, which he described as a psychological state where one has moved beyond a normal thought process and into a deep, almost trance-like concentration and feeling of connectedness. A flow state can induce feelings of ecstasy and clarity.

The structure and culture of a traditional corporate job may feel discouraging and stifling to many highly sensitive people. Yet many of my HSP clients have found joy in those corporate positions that require deep attention to detail, the creation of meaningful relationships, or new business structures and strategies in a wide range of industries such as insurance, law, finance, or sales.

One of my HSP clients, Josh, works for a national small-business loan company. Though his monthly sales quotas bring him a degree of stress, he has thrived nonetheless by using his HSP trait of being able to easily connect with his sales clients and staff and therefore establish lasting business relationships. He also utilizes his highly sensitive trait of paying close attention to detail when poring over customers' accounts to help create more financial opportunity for them.

The finely tuned intuition of many highly sensitive people can help them figure out what they desire to do, but they can also feel pressured by family or societal norms to do something else.

For example, Andrea, one of my HSP clients, chose a career path in medicine and academia largely due to pressure from her family and more broad cultural expectations. Though she excelled academically—and was valedictorian of her class at an Ivy League school—she did not enjoy what she did. She reported feeling bored, depressed, disconnected, and overwhelmed by the demands of her career. After some beautiful work in which she learned about and honored her HSP trait, she bravely claimed her creative talents, decided on a career change, and returned to school to study graphic design. She is currently growing a thriving freelance-based graphic design business where she works with nonprofit clients and feels like she can help others through her visual creativity.

Let's take some time now to assess your current job, career, or vocation choice(s) and, if you'd like, explore suitable work for your HSP nature.

Remember that one's vocation and how one pays the bills can be entirely separate entities. Some highly sensitive people, myself included, have had side jobs that "paid the bills" as we grew into our chosen careers and vocations.

## So What Do You Want to Be When You Grow Up?

If you are uncertain about the career or vocation that is best for you, this exercise can begin your exploration, particularly if you've never been given an opportunity to look more deeply at what it is you like. Think about that age-old question: What do you want to be when you "grow up"? What would you prefer doing if you did not have financial, family, and cultural pressures? Ask yourself these questions:

- What subjects am I naturally drawn to? What subjects excite me?

- How did I play as a child? Who did I pretend to be?

- In what ways was I not allowed to play or express myself? (If you're male, for example, were you discouraged from playing a nurse or teacher? If you're female, were you discouraged from playing a mechanic or doctor?)

- Did my family push me, either consciously or unconsciously, toward a career I did not actually feel connected to?

- What TV shows or movies do I enjoy most? Reality? Mystery? Game shows? What excites me both creatively and cognitively?

- In looking at my Instagram or Facebook accounts, who, what, and where do I follow the most?

- Do my vocation and how I make a living need to be the same or can they exist separately?

Your answers to these questions can help guide what you might truly want in a job or career but have not yet had the opportunity to express. Take as much time as you need to reflect and write your answers.

# Assessment

A change in a job or career may not be practical or even what's called for to better honor your HSP trait. Sometimes it's most beneficial to make adjustments, if possible, to our current work situation. These questions will help guide a deeper inquiry into whether changes related to your current work situation would better serve you.

- What do I like about my job? Am I working in something that feels like a calling?

- Does my work make me feel restored? Drained?

- How much or how little social structure does my work have? Can my HSP nature be honored in this situation?

- Do I get to experience flow? Is experiencing flow in my work important to me?

- Can I progress in my vocation? Is moving up important to me?

- Am I able to connect to my intuition in my workplace? Are my observations respected and honored?

- If I were able to choose any career, money and responsibilities aside, would I still be doing what I do now?

- Do I ever feel like I need to hide who I am to get through a workday?

- Do I ever fantasize about having a different career?

Based on your answers to the assessment questions, see if it is possible to make any changes in your current work situation to better suit your HSP nature. If you answered "yes" to the last question, the following exercise will help you further explore what your new chosen career will look and feel like.

## Living the "HSP Dream": A Day in the Working Life

Using your fabulous and deep imagination allow yourself to create the perfect HSP career or vocation for yourself. From the moment you open your gorgeous little highly sensitive eyes until that moment of relief when work is done, allow your imagination to take you through a typical, but highly pleasurable, workday. Some questions to consider:

- What career have I chosen?

- With whom, what, and where do I get to work?

- What is the quality of my work schedule, flexibility, and commute? Would I prefer a more structured nine-to-five or non-traditional work hours?

- Do I work for a small, medium, or large company? Or, do I own my own business?

- How much human interaction do I get daily?

- What does my downtime or vacation time look like?

- Do I get a real break or do I eat an overpriced salad at my desk for lunch?

- How do I feel at the end of the day? Tired? Fulfilled? Creatively satisfied?

After you have completed writing about your ideal day at work, see if you can seek out someone who has a career or work life you admire or would like to have. The following bonus strategy can assist you.

## Bonus Strategy

Interview or connect with a (preferably HSP) professional who has a career that looks appealing to you. This can look like a request for an informal informational interview or perhaps just a simple email exchange. Because highly sensitive people can be prone to perfectionism or can encounter difficulty with making mistakes, hearing the process and mistakes others have made along the way when moving into a chosen profession can be valuable. Highly sensitive people tend to be natural helpers so some will likely be happy to share their experiences with you.

# HIGHLY SENSITIVE PEOPLE IN THE WORKPLACE: HONORING YOUR SENSITIVITY AND AVOIDING BURNOUT

Though highly sensitive people can thrive in the workplace when our needs are met, many of us struggle under the demands and certain office conditions (think 24/7 access or the dreaded open-plan workplace). These difficulties can inhibit us from performing at our full potential.

Having our needs met and talents acknowledged in the workplace is so important. Can you imagine how many more innovations, creations, and solutions would take place if all highly sensitive people were provided with the conditions that made working ideal?

If your workplace is not ideal but you like aspects of your job, what tools or strategies can you utilize to make your circumstances more manageable? How can you create an environment that helps prevent exhaustion and burnout?

Bergsma found that 75 percent of the highly sensitive people who partici-pated in their study—a shockingly high rate—self-reported feeling burnout. A majority of participants reported feeling overwhelmed multiple times a day and struggled with exhaustion, concentration, and having "too many" thoughts. Over half reported feeling underappreciated by their superiors and fellow staff.

Many highly sensitive people picked up extra work and helped out, likely due to their deeply empathetic natures. They also tended to absorb and respond more to the emotions of their colleagues, work longer hours, and take fewer breaks than their less sensitive colleagues. The highly sensitive people also became more easily overwhelmed or exhausted by sensory and emotional factors in part because they tended to notice more details, which in turn flooded their highly sensitive nervous systems with too much stimuli. Finally, they reported struggling with workplace social situations and criticism more so than their less sensitive counterparts did.

The following sections offer some tools and strategies for assessing your workplace to see where shifts may occur to create a more HSP-friendly workplace.

## Assessing Your Workplace

As you move through the following questions, consider the structure and reality of your workplace culture. How can you work within your already existing workplace system to enact change?

- What can I realistically change and what is it necessary that I tolerate?
- Will I have support from my superiors and peers to make the changes I want?
- What realistic steps can I take now to help me feel more regulated in my workplace? What are my short-term goals? Long-term goals?

The leading challenge I see for many of my HSP clients is the open-plan workplace.

## Open-Plan Workplace Survival Guide

Though the open-plan workplace may seem ideal for collaboration and open communication among colleagues, this layout can actually be quite challenging for highly sensitive people because of the lack of privacy and constant stimulation. Here are some survival tips:

**REQUEST TO SIT IN A CORNER:** A corner seat, just like the aisle on an airplane, can offer more space in which to move and adjust. And in the corner, there is normally only one other nervous system to pick up on nearby as opposed to two when in a middle spot. The corner also creates an easy exit in case you need to regulate your nervous system during the workday.

**BLOCK IT OUT:** Because our highly sensitive nervous systems can have a stronger response to such stimuli as lights, smells, and noises, noise-canceling headphones are a must. Sunglasses or blue-blocking glasses, white noise machines, earplugs, soft (weighted if you'd like) blankets, or a scarf can also come in handy.

**CREATE A WALL, DOOR, OR HEDGE AROUND YOUR DESK:** Setting up a visual barrier can mimic a feeling of separation if you don't have an actual office door. Decorate the perimeter of your desk with art, plants, or objects you like. Or if you happen to work in a cubicle, consider purchasing a small gate or door.

**MAKE IT NICE:** One of the gifts of the highly sensitive person is the ability to deeply enjoy all things of beauty, whether art, nature, or those we love. Create a desk and workspace that is aesthetically pleasing to you. Having some leafy friends (aka plants!) can be especially calming and soothing.

**SCHEDULE "OFFICE HOURS":** Many open-plan workplaces fortunately have conference or small office spaces that can be utilized for meetings. If your workplace allows, see if you can reserve a private office space daily, weekly, or monthly to give yourself a break from the open plan.

If you feel it would benefit you to speak to your boss or superiors about changing your work environment to suit your highly sensitive nature, I would recommend focusing the conversation on what you need to be most efficient and productive rather than on your sensitivity. You can avoid confronting a situation where others misunderstand what it means to be a highly sensitive person this way.

## Working with Humans

Though highly sensitive people are talented at attuning to others and communicating, we can sometimes feel frustrated or misunderstood if someone does not understand us or is judgmental of our needs and sensitive natures. Here are some strategies to help you better educate those you work with.

**Find an HSP professional ally or community.** Especially within certain workplaces, it's more than likely that another highly sensitive person is in your workplace already! Using your keen intuition, seek out another highly sensitive person in your workplace. This can be someone to process, commiserate, or create strategies with. Some professions, especially those in the helping and creative fields, attract highly sensitive people.

***Communicate formally or informally about what it means to be highly sensitive.***

**Formally:**

- Offer to provide a training for your co-workers on highly sensitive people. Multiple resources on Elaine Aron's website, HSPerson.com, can provide the information you might need to do a basic educational training. If you go this route, I encourage you to focus more on the strengths that highly sensitive people can bring to the workplace and less on the "weaknesses."

- If your boss or human resources department seems hesitant about allowing a workshop, emphasize that the happier a highly sensitive person is in the workplace, the more productive they are, so it's to their and the company's benefit to give the green light.

- Hire a therapist knowledgeable about highly sensitive people to provide the training. Some HSP therapists also have online platforms you may be able to utilize.

- Offer to show the movie *Sensitive: The Untold Story* to your colleagues or send them the link (SensitiveTheMovie.com) to watch at their leisure.

- If you have found an HSP ally at work, see if you can collaborate on any initiatives to bring more information about highly sensitive people to your workplace.

**Informally:**

- If you feel anxious about introducing the topic of high sensitivity to colleagues, practice with trusted friends and family first.

- Create an HSP "elevator speech," meaning a quick one-minute introduction about highly sensitive people and invite others to hear more if they desire.

- Education about highly sensitive people can also occur within simple conversations with colleagues in meetings, office functions, or events outside work. Maybe you can arrange an HSP happy hour?

**Work with countertransference or strong emotional responses.** Therapists (this one included) are trained to be aware of countertransference, or the tendency to absorb someone else's distressing response as our own. Basically, if a client walks into my office extremely angry, I might absorb and feel that anger long after they have left my office. I find this phenomenon can also occur among co-workers as well, and we may not be fully aware of what we've absorbed until we investigate.

So, when you notice a strong emotional response in yourself, first accept it, be curious about it, and ask the simple question, *Is this response mine or someone else's?* As you continue to sit with your thoughts and feelings, you may find the emotions are not yours at all, but something you absorbed from another person. Practice "Developing Awareness of a Regulated and Calm Nervous System" and "Learning to Soothe: Working with Our 'Self-Cleaning Oven'" skills (pages 18–19). This work can help move difficult feelings through your nervous system.

**Develop curiosity, compassion, or firm boundaries with a difficult co-worker or boss.** Some humans are just difficult to work with! For these folks, use your traits of empathy and inquiry to play detective. Be curious about why this person might be difficult or hard to work with. Also utilize your skill of "Reframing Difficult Situations" (see page 24) to see if making internal adjustments is possible to reduce suffering around this person.

## TAKEAWAYS

Many highly sensitive people struggle with finding a job, career, or vocation that suits them. Explore and question what you learned about your own intelligence, traits, and talents to uncover what type of work feeds your soul or is possibly even your calling. But please remember your career or vocation and how you make a living can be separate entities!

Self-advocacy and honoring your HSP trait (see page 79) can make your workplace more HSP friendly. Please remember, though, that sometimes we cannot shift no matter how much we try and we will need to utilize the skill of "Learning to Soothe" to help manage our highly sensitive nervous systems. This can also create an opportunity to practice "Developing Awareness of a Regulated and Calm Nervous System," when needed.

Working with other humans can be challenging but we can utilize our highly sensitive traits to make it a happier and smoother work experience for everyone. Practice compassion for yourself and others.

# CHAPTER SIX

# Maintenance and Growth: The Care and Feeding of Highly Sensitive People

Caring for our highly sensitive selves while maintaining and balancing all the parts of our life can be a challenge. Because we tend to take in the world at a higher frequency and have heightened responses, we need to be mindful of how we care for our emotional, physical, and spiritual bodies.

This chapter focuses on maintaining equilibrium and taking care of our highly sensitive selves. We examine common health challenges of highly sensitive people. Additionally, we delve into the spiritual life of the highly sensitive person for ways to enrich our souls.

# FINDING OUR HOMEOSTASIS

Unlike some of our comparatively less sensitive peers, many highly sensitive people are able to find homeostasis, or a state of equilibrium, despite going against what's expected of us. For example, many of my clients who have chosen artistic pursuits—acting, music, writing, design—despite advice to make more "practical" choices, have found those pursuits highly meaningful to them.

Highly sensitive people can be attracted to "unconventional" ways of living. One of my clients, Dana, wrestled for years with the question of whether to have children. After much contemplation, she realized that she had always known deep down that she never wanted children. She felt she had been blind to her own intuition because she was taught that women should desire to be mothers. She felt tremendous relief and freedom once she was able to connect to her authentic needs.

Those needs can be undermined in the world of social media and its messages of perfection. Many highly sensitive people can find that social media leads them to compare themselves with others and as a result to experience judgment and suffering. Highly sensitive people can successfully navigate the social media world by asking themselves what they truly need and value to neutralize some of these effects.

As you begin to practice some of the skills and strategies in this book, be wary of the HSP tendency toward perfectionism. You may have unrealistic expectations about making changes in yourself and your relationships. Keep reading. "Intentional Mistake Making: Breaking the Habit of Perfectionism" (page 90) provides a strategy for learning to tolerate things not always going perfectly.

Be kind to yourself regarding your expectations and ability to effect changes in your environment.

## Discover Core Values

Discovering and honoring our core values will inform how we want to curate our lives authentically and what kind of focus and balance feels best for us. This work can also highlight areas that might need more care, attention, or concentration.

The following list contains ten core values that may align with your needs as a highly sensitive person. On a scale from 1 to 10, rate how significant each value is to you, with 10 being the most important and 1 being the least. Be sure to note any self-judgment or internalized value system you might be imposing on yourself as you list your core values.

_____ Money/Finances

_____ Romantic Relationships

_____ Family Relationships

_____ Self-identity

_____ Religion/Spirituality

_____ Art/Music

_____ Nature/Animals

_____ Communication/Honesty/Authenticity

_____ Physical Health/ Exercise

_____ Social/Global Justice

Once you have pinpointed your core values, use them as a guiding light to structure your life and align your personal priorities. The next exercise will enable you to focus even deeper on your core values and, along with the sensitive core skills, how to make them a reality in your life.

## Refining and Expanding Core Values

After you have identified your core values from the previous exercise, list them in descending order from 10 to 1 to see which are most important to you. Compare the values with the following nine core skills. What sensitive core skills might help you the most in the areas most valuable to you?

1. Self-advocacy/Self-parenting

2. Developing Awareness of Overstimulation

3. Developing Awareness of a Regulated and Calm Nervous System

4. Learning to Soothe

5. Developing Awareness of Emotions

6. Honoring and Responding to Truth and Justice

7. Honoring and Developing Joy and Creativity

8. Setting and Tolerating Boundaries

9. Reframing Difficult Situations

For example, if romantic relationships is one of your top values, then the skills of "Developing Awareness of Emotions: Naming, Allowing, and Processing Feelings" (see page 20) and "Setting and Tolerating Boundaries" (see page 23) might be a place to focus your attention. Or, if social and global justice is high on your list of values, focus on the skill of "Honoring and Responding to Truth and Justice" (see page 21) to see if it may need some care and attention. Mix and play with the core skills to explore what might help honor and strengthen the values most important to you.

## Intentional Mistake Making: Breaking the Habit of Perfectionism

Highly sensitive people often want to do a task correctly and well the first time (i.e., perfectionism). Though perfectionism isn't always a bad thing, this drive can hinder a highly sensitive person from approaching new experiences and making mistakes, an important part of learning and experiencing new things.

This is a gentle practice in tolerating mistakes and the thoughts and physical sensations that accompany them. Feel free to think of a "mistake" to make, but here are some suggestions.

Part 1:

• Intentionally order something incorrectly at a restaurant or fast food place. Once you receive your food, gently let them know you made a mistake and to please correct your order.

• Take the wrong way home from school or work. Once you have intentionally made this mistake, course correct, and continue your route.

- Drop, spill, or knock something over. A plastic cup full of water works well for this exercise.

- Mismatch your socks or other pieces of clothing you would normally match together.

Part 2:
- As best you can, allow yourself to feel the discomfort of your mistake.

- Track and note the thoughts, feelings, and sensations you are having, without judgment! What thoughts were you having before, during, and after the mistake? What physical sensations did you experience as it was happening? Were they uncomfortable but tolerable?

Part 3:
Ask yourself these questions:

- Was I uncomfortable for a temporary amount of time, or will this feeling last the rest of my days on earth?

- Did I die?

- Do all people and all living beings hate me now?

- Did the earth open up and swallow me whole?

- Bonus: What "mistake" did I make in the past that I was able to resolve, or that turned out okay?

Continue to explore these questions and see if maybe, just maybe, some mistakes can feel tolerable. Uncomfortable yes, but tolerable.

# HEALTHY, HAPPY HIGHLY SENSITIVE PEOPLE

The physical body holds and tells the story of emotional states and past traumas. For highly sensitive people who experience more deeply, making physical and emotional health—a holistic view—a priority is key.

In *The Empath's Survival Guide,* Dr. Judith Orloff says that highly sensitive people are more prone to what she calls *empathic illnesses* with somatic (biological) symptoms that do not originate in the highly sensitive person's brain or body. In fact, she calls them *physical empaths* or people who take on physical symptoms of another. These individuals might view themselves as having psychological diagnoses such as anxiety or panic disorders, depression, or chronic fatigue or pain. Dr. Orloff found that these individuals do not respond to usually effective forms of treatment but find healing by less standard means such as finding more alone time, spending time in nature, or developing a meditation practice.

Dr. Orloff also points out that highly sensitive people are more prone to binge eating to decrease feelings of emotional overwhelm and that we are tempted toward more comforting food, especially sugar, carbs, or any junk food. I personally resonate with this tendency deeply. Despite the many other soothing, calming, and healing modalities I have practiced, I have found deep joy in a Taco Bell bean and cheese burrito with gobs of hot sauce. This soothing bundle can sometimes bring me as much pleasure and comfort as a warm bath or a soothing hug. The warm embrace of refried beans enveloped by the hot and soothing tingle of hot sauce calms my highly sensitive soul like no other.

The unique relationship to the physical and emotional health of the highly sensitive person was also discussed in an illuminating post on Elaine Aron's blog, *Comfort Zone,* published in 2014. Dr. Aron discusses the concept of *eudaimonia,* a concept Aristotle explored which he describes as pleasure one experiences when they are doing what they were meant to do.

Aristotle's theories were later confirmed by a 2008 study published in the National Academy of Sciences. Researchers discovered that certain areas of our gene structures could increase or decrease the activity and strength of the immune system and inflammatory responses, depending on one's behavior and feeling state. Happier people had stronger immune systems and less inflammation in their bodies. A happy, fulfilled, and meaningful life cannot necessarily shield us from pain and disease, but the research shows it can certainly help!

Because highly sensitive people are more prone to experience trauma and symptoms related to traumatic experiences, we are more likely to develop physical or chronic illnesses expressed in our bodies in response to trau-matic experiences. These can appear as addictions, autoimmune diseases, sleep disturbances, or mental health difficulties. As a highly sensitive person, you may be familiar with how your emotional self is closely linked to your physical one and how one may influence the other.

## TIPS TO KEEP YOUR HIGHLY SENSITIVE SELF AS HAPPY AND HEALTHY AS HUMANLY POSSIBLE

- Make mental health a priority. As we have just discussed, a happy highly sensitive person is a healthy highly sensitive person. Please remember that as much as we might like to, we cannot disconnect our emotional state from our physical one. Taking care of our emotional and psychological needs is equally as if not more important for a highly sensitive person.

- Recognize that if we are under stress or have experienced a recent trauma, we are far more likely to develop an illness because of our natural psychosomatic natures. If you have experienced or are currently experiencing a stressful or traumatic situation, take extra care of your emotional and physical being. Be mindful and kind to yourself if you do get sick as a response to a difficult or traumatic situation. Being judgmental or cruel to yourself will not help you heal.

- Though this has yet to be critically studied, I, and many highly sensitive therapists in my highly sensitive therapists community, surmise that highly sensitive people are more prone to addiction, such as drugs, alcohol, sex, and gambling. Any addiction at its core provides tools for calming, soothing, and emotional regulation. If you are struggling with an addiction, help is available. Most insurance plans cover addiction treatment and many states in the United States provide free or low-cost treatments for those who are struggling.

- Food sensitivities and allergies are very common for highly sensitive people. If you are unsure of your exact sensitivities, consider being tested. Most general practitioners can provide allergy testing so that you have the information you need to honor and balance your highly sensitive body. The core sensitive skill of "Self-advocacy/Self-parenting" (see page 15) is also important in this circumstance, in that we may have to ask for special accommodations to fit our dietary restrictions.

- Move that beautiful, sensitive body if you can on a daily basis. I cannot emphasize enough the importance of incorporating movement into your self-care routine. The focus is not on weight loss but on moving the body in a way that increases our endorphins. High Intensity Interval Training (HIIT) or yoga are two great options. A little sweat is a great release for the highly sensitive body. Even a short daily walk can do wonders.

- Our highly sensitive systems are more prone to autoimmune disorders and chronic pain if we have also experienced trauma, especially during childhood. Beyond working with your regular doctors, consider working with a therapist or healer who combines body and psychological work. Somatic experiencing, created by the brilliant Peter Levine, is a method that works exclusively with the body and can be a powerful healing method for both soul and body. Psychomotor and Mindfulness-Based Cognitive Therapy are also modalities to consider.

- Because the highly sensitive system can be more susceptible to environment and food, we might also have a sensitivity to some, or all, medications as well. If you are prescribed a medication, discuss with your provider your high sensitivity and whether lower doses of medications might be just as effective for you.

## Advocating for Your Highly Sensitive Mind and Body

Because our healthcare system is not necessarily built for the highly sensitive person, we may occasionally need to advocate for our needs in a medical setting. Many of us also tend toward "invisible" conditions that are chronic or affect the autoimmune system. Doctors and other health-care practitioners may not have a full understanding of the cause of our illness, requiring more self-advocating.

For example, my client, Olivia, has polycystic ovarian syndrome (aka PCOS), a hormonal disorder that can cause many health issues such as irregular periods, fatigue, infertility, insulin resistance, weight gain, depression, and risk for other health problems such as diabetes and high blood pressure. During her yearly checkup with her general practitioner, a small nodule was found on her thyroid that needed further testing. She was referred to a specialist to investigate.

At her first appointment, the specialist examined her thyroid and they reviewed her history, including her PCOS diagnosis. Without Olivia inquiring about this particular subject, the doctor began to tell Olivia about a weight loss plan she should try, and what kind of exercise plan she should be doing. Olivia quietly listened, being familiar with doctors lecturing her about weight loss, even though she had been dieting since she was a teenager. The doctor also recommended weight loss medica-tion. Olivia was puzzled because she had also mentioned a history of eating disorders to the doctor. Given her circumstances, it seemed a bit of an extreme recommendation, especially after only 10 minutes. Olivia nodded along to the lecture, said no, thank you, to the weight loss medication recommendation, got an ultrasound order for her thyroid, and left, processing her anger and frustration later in our session that day.

In her follow-up appointment, Olivia looked forward to getting the results of her ultrasound. She learned the first results were inconclusive and she would need to be tested again. As if they had never had the first conversation, the doctor again lectured Olivia about the same diet and exercise plan and suggested the same weight loss medication. Olivia again chose to sit back and listen because she was too angry to respond the way she really wanted to. A couple of days after the appointment, Olivia spent her free moments thinking deeply about her response, penned an email to her doctor, and calmly but firmly explained how being lectured not once but twice was insulting and not needed. She also took the opportunity to let her know that this way of communicat-ing with patients, especially sensitive ones, was disrespectful and unhelpful. Using her gifts of gentle strength and clear communication,

Olivia was successfully able to voice her feelings and experiences. Her doctor soon wrote back with an apology and the promise to focus just on her thyroid nodule through the rest of her treatment.

Unfortunately, Olivia's story of not feeling heard or understood by a medical professional resonates with many highly sensitive people. Think back to a time where you felt similarly about a situation you had with a doctor. If you could go back in time and confront them, what would you say? How could you use some of your new skills to advocate for yourself? Or, if you could write them an email to confront them, what would you want them to know? How would you like your treatment to look?

## Consider Holistic Healing Modalities

As highly sensitive people, we have a deep mind-body connection. It can be helpful to consider alternative ways of healing that involve more holistic or sensory-based methods. Because our nervous systems are more open and susceptible to stimuli, I suspect that highly sensitive people may have better results in more sensory-based healing modalities due to our bodies' and nervous systems' abilities to take in more sensory information when looking for ways to care and heal. Consider some of these modalities:

- Acupuncture

- Aromatherapy

- Art Therapy

- Craniosacral Manipulation

- Emotional Freedom Technique, also known as Tapping

- Meditation (especially mindful meditation and transcendental meditation)

- Nature Therapy

- Reiki

- Shiatsu Massage

- Sound Healing

Not every healing modality works for everyone, and some are more appropriate for different times and needs.

# Daily HSP Health Tips: Am I Fed and Watered?

- Highly sensitive people are prone to neglecting their basic needs, especially when they are under time restraints, anxiety, or stress. This is a counterintuitive response because when we do not meet our basic needs, more stress and inflammation are created in the body. This neglect makes difficult and stressful situations that much harder.

- Check in with your basic needs at least three times a day. One way to do this is to put a reminder in your workspace, in your phone, or anywhere you'll see the reminder frequently. Ask yourself these simple, but critical, questions:

   Are you fed?

   Are you watered?

   How much or how little caffeine have you had today?

   Are you tired?

   How are you feeling emotionally?

   How does your body feel?

   Do you have an "emotional hangover?" (being tired from a strong emotional response from the day before)

   Have you taken a deep breath today?

   Have you connected with nature today?

   Have you moved your body today?

   Have you connected with someone you care about today?

   Have you witnessed or listened to something beautiful or pleasurable?

- If you feel you lack in any of those areas, tend to yourself. Grab a snack, have some water, take a nap, hug a tree, find a dog or cat to pet, turn on some good music, or take a deep belly breath. Your highly sensitive mind and body will thank you!

# SELF-CARE FOR THE SENSITIVE

The practice and modeling of self-care is incredibly present in our current culture. Splashed across our social media timelines, TV screens, and phone advertisements images of bubble baths, face masks, and messages of treating yourself bombard us. Though there is certainly nothing wrong with a good bubble bath, highly sensitive people must prioritize self-care in ways that may be different from our less sensitive peers. Because highly sensitive people have the tendency to be more empathetic, we can be more likely to neglect our own needs to be in the service of others.

No matter how many yoga classes you take, hours you meditate, or pounds of organic food you have eaten, these actions will be far less impactful if you do not have a kind and healthy relationship with yourself. Beating yourself up over something you perceive you did not do well or anything else will not help. Know that it is certainly not your fault if you do have negative self-talk because these voices in our minds get created over time and are based on the explicit or implicit messages we receive about ourselves. The number one tool for self-care is treating yourself with respect, kindness, and care. This is especially important if you have only just begun a journey of healing and are still learning about your authentic self.

## Internalized Self-care: Back to Kindergarten

A helpful metaphor I use with my clients is thinking about the interior of your mind as the interior of a kindergarten classroom. Part of you is an observer; another part, the teacher; and still another, the young, sensitive student who is open to both negative and positive messages.

Kindergarten classrooms and kindergarten teachers are ideal for highly sensitive people. The kindergarten classroom is a colorful, inviting environment where snack and nap time is always on the agenda. A typical kindergarten teacher will also have a kind and compassionate tone with her students, even if they make mistakes.

They won't say, "Hey there, a**hole, color between the lines!" They might gently point out the student's creativity and offer other solutions. These learning environments are designed with the intention that these little humans learn best when they feel safe, calm, loved, and accepted.

As highly sensitive humans of any age, we can still benefit from creating an internal environment where we are welcome and safe, even if we decide to color outside the lines a bit and take a little longer rest at nap time. If you find you are speaking to yourself harshly or negatively, see if you can practice embodying the nature and tone of your internalized kindergarten teacher.

For example: You make a mistake on an important report for work. Your mind and thoughts might initially sound like this: *You idiot, how could you make that mistake? You moron, what is wrong with you? You don't do anything right!*

See if you can reword the message into something kinder, gentler, more kindergarten teacher like. Maybe, *Well, my darling perfectly imperfect human, you seem to have made a mistake with this. You may want to review what you did and see if you can do a better job next time. Would you like a snack?*

It is possible to manage a difficult moment, such as making a mistake, without harsh and, frankly, unhelpful words. You are not sparing yourself the responsibility; you are acknowledging that it is possible to learn and grow without having to berate yourself constantly.

If you find you are having difficulty speaking or relating to yourself with kindness and respect, discussing this with your therapist or healer, if you hopefully have one, would be extremely beneficial. If you do not have a therapist or healer and would like one, the following section can assist you in finding one.

## How to Find a (Highly Sensitive Knowledgeable) Therapist or Healer

As a psychotherapist, I am constantly asked by friends, family, or people I just met how to find a therapist. Here is a handy guide for finding a therapist or healer who understands your highly sensitive nature.

- One of the greatest acts of self-care is the gift of healing. Though 50 percent of highly sensitive people are already in psychotherapy (Aron 2010), for those who are not, finding someone who understands their highly sensitive nature can be an overwhelming prospect. It is, however, absolutely doable.

- Elaine Aron includes a listing of HSP-knowledgeable therapists, coaches, and medical professionals, listed by US state and also outside the United States on her website, HSPerson.com. Hopefully you can find an HSP knowledgeable therapist near you. If not, more and more therapists are now licensed in multiple states and may be able to provide phone or video sessions remotely.

- I caution you: No matter how wonderful someone's Instagram or Facebook page might look, or how deeply you resonate with their inspirational memes, do not—I repeat, do not—work with anyone who is unlicensed by a state or medical body, even if they proclaim they "specialize" in highly sensitive people. I have witnessed too many social media, self-proclaimed self-help "coaches" online, who do not have real credentials or training to work with the complexities of the human condition. Plenty of help by actual professionals is available. That said, spiritual, intuitive, and some alternative modes of healing do not have official licensure bodies at this time. If you feel these practitioners could be a benefit to you, make sure you adequately vet the healer's experience and training.

- Ask friends or family whom you trust if they know of any good therapists or have enjoyed their experience with any particular therapist in the past. If you are lucky to have a loved one who is a therapist in your life, ask them for recommendations.

- Consider what traits you would like your ideal therapist to have. Some aspects to consider are gender identity, age, level of experience, specialties, certifications, and therapeutic perspective. There is no right or wrong answer, just what feels best and most comfortable for you.

- If you have the means, go therapist shopping! I suggest when narrowing down the search to pick your top three, then contact each via an email or phone call. Most therapists generally provide free 15-to-20-minute consultations during which you can speak about your needs and find out how the therapist works with their clients. If you like and have the time and funds, make an initial, in-person, appointment with each therapist. The best way to determine whether this therapist is best for you is to see if you feel seen, heard, safe, and comfortable speaking with them in the therapeutic space.

- Ask your possible new therapist if they have done their own personal psychotherapy. I consider it a must that a therapist does their own healing work if they are going to help others. If they refuse to tell you, or say they have not done their own work, I highly advise that you not work with that person.

- Do not take it personally or relinquish your search if a therapist does not get back to you or is very delayed in returning your initial inquiry. Many therapists, especially highly sensitive ones in private practice like me, sometimes cannot get back to new clients as quickly as we would like. Our job, though incredibly meaningful and rewarding, can be extremely exhausting, and tasks like answering emails or phone calls sometimes can fall through the cracks. If you feel drawn to working with a particular therapist, feel free to follow up with them if you have not heard back in a timely manner. I personally, as a therapist, never mind if a new client follows up with me if I have yet to get back to them

- If you do not have insurance or are low on funds, consider seeing a therapist at a university or at a group therapy practice with therapists-in-training, gathering their client contact (face-to-face client time) hours for licensure. These therapists-in-training are always supervised by experienced licensed therapists who are also specially trained to teach and provide supervision to beginning therapists through their state licensing board. You will most likely get a high-quality level of care at a much lower cost.

- If you are already in therapy, please feel empowered to ask your current therapist if they know about highly sensitive people and are willing to explore the HSP trait with you, or perhaps even get some knowledge or training around it, if they do not have this training already. If your therapist expresses any bias or judgment toward highly sensitive people, seriously consider switching to a different therapist.

# Self-care for the Highly Sensitive Helper and Healer

Because highly sensitive people are natural or professional helpers and healers, I felt compelled to include a section on self-care for healers, for as much as we preach it, we tend to have difficulty practicing it for ourselves.

- Please remember that no matter how gifted we are, no matter how many people pull on our coats begging for help, no matter how much our hearts break in wanting to assist every broken heart and aching soul in the world, we are humans first, healers second. As much as we may be tempted not to, we must always acknowledge our own humanity. Isn't that what we are trying to teach when we are helping others? Good healers don't teach others to be indestructible robots; they teach them to work within their own human condition. Practice what you so exquisitely preach.

- Though it may seem obvious, please remember we do not have to save everything and everyone, even when we feel we may be of service to the situation. Particularly remember this when you as a healer or helper need to take care of yourself, physically or mentally, or temporarily step away from your practice, or change the type of clients or patients you work with. Also, as much as this may feel like a blow to the ego, we are not the only one who can be of assistance, even though it may appear that way on the surface. Though this fact may sting momentarily, it frees us from feeling the pressure to assist when we already know we are stretched to our limits. Refer out if you need to.

- Become conscious of why you feel compelled to help or heal others. Yes, it can be part of our vocation or calling to be of service, but I have found that all healers do have at least a part of themselves getting healed by helping. For some, it is to find value and meaning in themselves when they previously did not feel that way. Though this truly is a beautiful thing, it is crucial to be cautious and conscious of why we feel so compelled to be there for others and how we may be sacrificing our own physical or mental health to heal that part of ourselves that feels unworthy.

- If you are training to be a therapist, or any kind of healer, please make sure your supervisor or mentor understands and respects your highly sensitive nature. Some doctors or therapists see the highly sensitive traits, though medically studied and proven, as a psychological fad. It is not, and if your current supervisor or mentor judges or challenges you on the validity of the traits, consider changing supervisors or finding a mentor who understands and values your highly sensitive nature.

# SPIRITUALITY FOR THE SENSITIVE SOUL

Psychiatrist, author, and Holocaust survivor, Victor Frankl wrote the heartbreaking and timeless *Man's Search for Meaning* in which he explores the survival of the human condition under the most horrific circumstances— Auschwitz, a Nazi concentration camp. He says, "Sensitive people who were used to a rich intellectual life may have suffered much pain (they were often of a delicate constitution), but the damage to their inner selves was less. They were able to retreat from their terrible surroundings to a life of inner riches and spiritual freedom. Only in this way can one explain the apparent paradox that some prisoners of a less hardy make-up often seemed to survive camp life better than did those of a robust nature."

I do wonder if Frankl was himself a highly sensitive person though this is not explicitly identified. It is possible that the strengths of his HSP trait helped him survive. There is an incredible fortitude and power that comes with our sensitivities, but sometimes we forget because we can be bogged down with information that focuses on the negatives of being a highly sensitive person. We may tend to focus more on our weaknesses and not on the tremendous vitality that we can bring to ourselves and the world.

I am the grandchild of Holocaust survivors. Both my paternal grandfather and grandmother endured the Holocaust, both as prisoners in Auschwitz. Sadly, because of their traumas and other unfortunate circumstances, I was never able to speak to my grandparents about their sensitivity, if they indeed possessed the traits. Did they also have a rich inner life and vivid imagination that kept them going during their horrendous experiences? Did they have a deep intuition or sense of knowing that helped them survive as they experienced the terror of the Holocaust? Sadly, I will never know for sure, but what I do know is I did inherit my own sensitivity from somewhere, possibly from them.

The following sections touch more deeply on the issue of spirituality and connecting with our deeper knowing, sometimes known as intuition. I will also briefly explain the shadow side of being a highly sensitive person. Know that many highly sensitive people, myself included, sometimes struggle with discovering and enriching one's spiritual life.

## Hearing Your Wisest Voice: Connecting with Intuition

One of the most precious gifts highly sensitive people have is our deep intuition. Though many of us can have a strong intuitive sense, some struggle with connecting to our wisest voice if we were wrongfully conditioned not to listen to it, generally beginning in childhood.

Though intuition never truly leaves us, we may need to relearn to hear and recognize how it shows up within our beings. Sometimes it is the gentle rumble in your belly that connects with a soft, quiet voice in your mind, gently guiding you. Or it shows up strongly, like a loud yell or siren, an internal GPS telling you to turn around or stop. You always have it with you. You just need to listen.

Here are some simple and safe ways to practice reconnecting with your intuition.

**TAKE AN INTUITIVE WALK:** Without deciding on a route, take an intuitive walk in your neighborhood. This means, without thinking (as best you can), follow the lead of your body and senses to let them tell you where you would like to go. The scent of a flower catch your nose? Get closer. A ray of light around the corner? See what's there. Hear some birds in the distance? Perhaps you want to follow their call. Listen to and closely observe your body's signals to determine which direction feels good to you.

**MAKE AN INTUITIVE ART PROJECT:** Bust out your crayons, markers, paint brushes, etc., and create some intuitive art. Quiet the mind as best you can, and let your hands and fingers lead the way. Let your eyes settle on the colors that feel right at that moment. There is no right or wrong, only what feels good. See what beauty you create!

**INTUIT AND CHILL:** Put on Netflix or any other streaming platform. As best you can, again without thinking, see if you can connect with your intuition to find something to watch that perhaps you have not seen before. Rather than pick what everyone else is watching, see if you can listen to that curious, quiet voice within to fulfill a curiosity you didn't even know was there.

After practicing connecting with your intuition, become familiar with what your intuition feels like in the body. It does give us subtle messages. In your journal, or anywhere you like, track your experience with your intuition. What does your intuition sound and feel like? Is there an image that comes to you? Does it sound like anything? Where in your body does it live? How can you create a clearer dialogue with it? See if you can begin to create a stronger relationship with your wisest inner guide.

## Connecting with Our Highly Sensitive Shadow

The concept of the shadow was developed by Swiss psychologist Carl Jung (who also wrote about sensitivity in his work!). As someone who bridged the gap between psychology and spirituality, he is unique in the field. Through his own studies of different realms of spirituality, and using his own deep imagination to anchor his ideas and concepts, Jung proposed that we all have a shadow, defined as a human being's "dark side," or the part of ourselves we want to keep in the shadows and not let anyone see, including ourselves (Aron 2004).

Elaine Aron also describes the shadow side of the HSP trait, defining it as weakness, the ability to be a doormat, indecisiveness, irritability, and having a critical nature toward others or the world (Aron 2005).

In my personal life and clinical practice, I find the most glaring shadow aspect of being a highly sensitive person is irritation, anger, and rage. Anger that we feel misunderstood, irritation that the world isn't always designed for our sensitive natures, and absolute rage that less sensitive people do not notice and see and experience the world the way we do.

I feel the only way to work with the shadow is to acknowledge, honor, and embrace it. If you have been taught your anger is wrong, I invite you to believe otherwise and find a way to welcome in the anger, see what it has to say, and if it needs to be expressed. Sometimes just allowing ourselves to feel our shadowy feelings, even if they feel "wrong" somehow, can begin to cool the flames of anger. Discuss this with your therapist or healer if you feel it could be helpful.

## DIY Spirituality

If you already have a connection to a religion or spiritual practice that works for you, please feel free to skip this section. If you feel a need to deepen your relationship with a higher purpose, or are compelled to begin a spiritual journey, please read on.

- If part of your childhood experience included organized religion and you felt it did resonate with your core principles and practices, see what you can do to expand your existing knowledge in a way that feels manageable to you. Perhaps you could read the Bible, Torah, or other religious text, or attend services once a week or month. But I implore you, please try your best not to let guilt slip in when you are exploring another spiritual path. This is your journey, no one else's.

- If you like, explore other organized religions beyond the one you were taught growing up. Perhaps you grew up in a Catholic household but never quite felt connected to its spiritual practices. Take some time to read and explore other organized religions such as Judaism or Buddhism. See what speaks to you.

- If you feel your soul does not resonate with organized religion, know that many feel this way. Empower yourself to explore other types of "alternative" spirituality, such as astrology, tarot, or connecting to your own psychic or intuitive abilities if you feel you possess them.

- Create your own spiritual well. This will be a place, book, center or practice you can return to and receive soul nourishment from when life becomes chaotic, overwhelming, or out of control. To be honest, at the moment, my DIY spiritual practice includes a daily yoga practice, podcasts I have discovered that, surprisingly, have given me deep connection and spiritual fulfillment, and spending as much time with animals and nature as I can. (My favorites are in the Resources section of this book; see page 111.) I also consider my work as a therapist to be a sacred and spiritual practice. Perhaps you can find spirituality and sacredness in your work as well.

# TAKEAWAYS

Discovering and honoring our core values as highly sensitive people can create a road map to creating a balanced and sustainable life. You are entitled and worthy of creating what feels authentic to you.

"Self-advocacy/Self-parenting" (see page 15) is an essential strategy for overall health and happiness. Continuously exercise and flex this vital muscle to get the quality of care you need and deserve. Be patient and compassionate with yourself as you discover and align your core values and begin to live them out.

Practicing and working with perfectionism is critical to a highly sensitive person's well-being and growth. Perfectionism may appear in your process. If so, please practice tolerating it within yourself.

Tending to mental health is key to a highly sensitive person's wellness because of our exquisite, mind-body connection. Know, too, that both your physical and psychological health deserve equal care and attention.

Self-care is also essential to our well-being, especially because many highly sensitive people are personal, and sometimes professional, helpers and healers. Care for yourself as well as you do for others.

If self-actualization or self-integration is important to you, honoring and working with the shadow aspects of the HSP trait can serve you greatly. All emotions are welcome!

# RESOURCES

## BOOKS

*The Highly Sensitive Child* by Elaine Aron, PhD
In *The Highly Sensitive Child*, Elaine Aron brings her expertise to the parents of highly sensitive children. She provides education, guidance, and insight as well as self-tests and case studies to help parents understand the unique needs of their highly sensitive child.

*The Highly Sensitive Person* and *The Highly Sensitive Person in Love* by Elaine Aron, PhD
Both of these books are a must-read for any highly sensitive human and a wonderful place to begin your education about highly sensitive people. *The Highly Sensitive Person in Love* is also a great resource to give to non-HSP partners who would like to learn more about the HSP trait.

*The Strong, Sensitive Boy* by Ted Zeff, PhD
*The Strong, Sensitive Boy* is a vital resource for any caregiver, parent, or teacher of a highly sensitive boy. It offers research, advice, and interventions. The book is also a great read for any highly sensitive man who might want a deeper insight into common struggles highly sensitive boys face.

## FILMS

*Sensitive: The Untold Story* and *Sensitive and in Love*: SensitiveTheMovie.com
Both these films are wonderful resources for taking a more in-depth look at what it is to be a highly sensitive person. *Sensitive* is a documentary-style film that explores the world from a highly sensitive point of view and includes interviews with Elaine Aron and musician Alanis Morissette. *Sensitive and in Love* presents the fictional story of siblings as they discover and work with their high sensitivity in a journey of healing and finding love.

### Won't You Be My Neighbor?

Examines the life and legacy of Fred Rogers and his irreplaceable children's program, *Mister Rogers' Neighborhood*, and is a must for any highly sensitive person, or truly, any human! This gorgeous and heart-filled documentary is the best film I have ever seen about childhood trauma, healing, and the human condition.

## PODCASTS

You can find these podcasts on SoundCloud, Spotify, or other streaming platforms.

### Ram Dass Here and Now

This podcast has been a surprising gift to me and is now part of my DIY spiritual practice. Gracefully gifted by the Love Serve Remember Foundation, this podcast is hosted by Raghu Markus who shares excerpted lectures by spiritual leader and psychologist Ram Dass, throughout the last 40 years of Dass's life. His works are timeless, deeply wise, spiritually freeing, and comforting.

### Unapologetically Sensitive

Patricia Young, LCSW and HSP coach, explores the strengths and challenges of the trait in this podcast. She provides 60 + episodes where she has in-depth conversations with experts in the field of healing, discussing issues that emerge for highly sensitive people, introverts, or those who identify as INFJ or ENFJ personality types.

### Very Ape Podcast

Documentarians and hosts Sean Dune and Cass Greener (*American Juggalo*, *Florida Man*, *Oxyana*), lovingly explore the worlds of consciousness, healing (sometimes through alternative means), art, love, music, and the human condition. The thing I appreciate most about this podcast is how Sean speaks about and models vulnerability and sensitivity and openly discusses his struggles as a man on a healing journey.

## WEBSITES

### HSPerson.com

If you are new to learning about the HSP trait, this website by Elaine Aron is a wonderful place to begin your journey. There are a number of HSP resources including the HSP Self-test; Elaine Aron's blog, *Comfort Zone*;

events; workshops; and access to a directory of HSP-knowledgeable therapists and other professionals.

## Meetup.com

This website is a great tool to find events geared for highly sensitive people
or to find a community of other highly sensitive people. Both online and
in-person connections are possible.

## SensitiveTherapist.com

SensitiveTherapist.com is a great resource for any therapist or healer with a
highly sensitive soul. Created by my wonderful colleague April Snow, LMFT,
the site provides invaluable resources, community, and support. April
also runs yearly Highly Sensitive Therapist retreats, which are an amazing
resource for HSP therapists to find support and community.

# YOUTUBE

## Lee Harris Energy

I learned about Lee Harris from a colleague at the first Highly Sensitive
Therapist retreat I attended. If you are curious about developing your intuition and connecting to a higher power beyond organized religion, I highly
recommend Lee. He often speaks about highly sensitive people and empaths
and displays gentle but strong and healing energy. He provides monthly and
yearly "Energy Updates" where he takes the pulse of what's happening for
individuals and the world around us. He also has a special interest in highly
sensitive and empathic, heart-centered entrepreneurs, and provides education and resources through his membership community. I have found him
informative, wise, and comforting during these current difficult times.

## Yoga with Adriene

Adriene Mishler is truly a gift to YouTube, yoga, and me! I discovered
Adriene on YouTube after many years of harsh exercise and an equally harsh
relationship with my body. In her incredibly welcoming, loving, funny, and
goofy, yet graceful, way, Adriene has hundreds of videos on her free channel
that cover an incredible array of topics. In addition to yoga, she also has
videos that focus on meditation and different forms of mindful breathing.
She has enabled me to build a daily yoga practice I can literally do anywhere,
for free! Also, her adorable dog Benji makes an appearance in many of her
videos. I cannot recommend her enough!

# REFERENCES

Acevedo, Bianca P., Elaine N. Aron, Arthur Aron, Matthew-Donald Sangster, Nancy Collins, and Lucy L. Brown. "The Highly Sensitive Brain: An fMRI Study of Sensory Processing Sensitivity and Response to Others' Emotions." *Brain and Behavior* 4, no. 4 (2014): 580–94. doi.org/10.1002/brb3.242.

Acevedo Bianca P., Elaine N. Aron, Sarah Pospos, and Dana Jessen. "The Functional Highly Sensitive Brain: A Review of the Brain Circuits Underlying Sensory Processing Sensitivity and Seemingly Related Disorders." *Philosophical Transactions of the Royal Society B: Biological Sciences* 373, no. 1744 (2018): 20170161. doi.org/10.1098/rstb.2017.0161.

Acevedo, Bianca P., Jadzia Jagiellowicz, Elaine N. Aron, Robert Marhenke, and Arthur Aron. "Sensory Processing Sensitivity and Childhood Quality's Effects on Neural Responses to Emotional Stimuli." *Clinical Neuropsychiatry* 14, no. 6 (December 2017): 359–73.

Aron, Elaine N. "The Clinical Implications of Jung's Concept of Sensitiveness." *Journal of Jungian Theory and Practice* 8, no. 2 (2006): 11–43. researchgate.net/publication/251399389_The_Clinical_Implications_of_Jung's_Concept_of_Sensitiveness.

———. "Why HSPs' Tendency to Worry about the Real Meaning of Our Life May Make Us Healthier." *Comfort Zone* (blog). The Highly Sensitive Person, June 15, 2014. hsperson.com/why-hsps-tendency-to-worry-about-the-real-meaning-of-our-life-may-make-us-healthier.

———. *The Highly Sensitive Child: Helping Our Children Thrive When the World Overwhelms Them.* New York: Harmony Books, 2015.

———. *The Highly Sensitive Person: How to Thrive When the World Overwhelms You.* Rev. ed. New York: Broadway Books, 2020.

———. *The Highly Sensitive Person in Love: Understanding and Managing Relationships When the World Overwhelms You.* New York: Harmony Books, 2001.

———. *Highly Sensitive Therapist Retreat.* Santa Cruz, CA, 2019.

——. "High Sensitivity as One Source of Fearfulness and Shyness: Preliminary Research and Clinical Implications." In *Extreme Fear, Shyness, and Social Phobia: Origins, Biological Mechanisms, and Clinical Outcomes,* edited by Louis A. Schmidt and Jay Schulkin, 251–72. New York: Oxford University Press, 1999.

——. "The Impact of Temperament on Intimacy and Closeness." In *Handbook of Closeness and Intimacy,* edited by Debra J. Mashek and Arthur Aron, 267–83. Mahwah, NJ: Lawrence Erlbaum Associates, 2004.

——. *Psychotherapy and the Highly Sensitive Person: Improving Outcomes for That Minority of People Who Are the Majority of Clients.* New York: Routledge, 2010.

——. "Revisiting Jung's Concept of Innate Sensitiveness." *Journal of Analytical Psychology* 49 (2004): 337–67.

——. "The Shadow Side to High Sensitivity." *Comfort Zone* (blog). The Highly Sensitive Person, August 28, 2005. hsperson.com/the-shadow-side-to -high-sensitivity.

Aron, Elaine N., and Arthur Aron. "Sensory-Processing Sensitivity and Its Relation to Introversion and Emotionality." *Journal of Personality and Social Psychology* 73, no. 2 (1997): 345–68. doi.org/10.1037/0022-3514.73.2.345.

Aron, Elaine N., Arthur Aron, and Kristin M. Davies. "Adult Shyness: The Interaction of Temperamental Sensitivity and an Adverse Childhood Environment." *Personality and Social Psychology Bulletin* 31, no. 2 (2005): 181–197. doi.org/10.1177/0146167204271419.

Aron, Elaine N., Arthur Aron, Natalie Nardone, and Shelly Zhou. "Sensory Processing Sensitivity and the Subjective Experience of Parenting: An Exploratory Study." *Family Relations* 68, no. 4 (2019): 420–35. doi.org/10.1111 /fare.12370.

Belsky, Jay, and Michael Pluess. "Beyond Diathesis Stress: Differential Susceptibility to Environmental Influences." *Psychological Bulletin* 135, no. 6 (2009): 885–908. doi.org/10.1037/a0017376.

Bergsma, Esther. "HSP and Burnout: International Research." Hoogsensitief.nl, January 9, 2019. hoogsensitief.nl/hsp-and-burnout-international-research.

Cain, Susan. *Quiet: The Power of Introverts in a World That Can't Stop Talking.* New York: Broadway Paperbacks, 2012.

Csikszentmihalyi, Mihaly. *Flow: The Psychology of Optimal Experience.* New York: HarperCollins, 1990.

De Villiers, Bernadette, Francesca Lionetti, and Michael Pluess. "Vantage Sensitivity: a Framework for Individual Differences in Response to Psychological Intervention." *Social Psychiatry and Psychiatric Epidemiology* 53, no. 6 (April 2018): 545–54. doi.org/10.1007/s00127-017-1471-0.

Frankl, Viktor. *Man's Search for Meaning: An Introduction to Logotherapy.* Boston: Beacon Press, 2012.

Frey, William H., and Muriel Langseth. *Crying: The Mystery of Tears.* Minneapolis, MN: Winston Press, 1985.

Harper, Will, dir. *Sensitive and in Love.* 2020; New York: The Global Touch Group.

Harper, Will, dir. *Sensitive: The Untold Story.* 2015; New York: The Global Touch Group.

Levine, Amir, and Rachel Heller. *Attached: Identify Your Attachment Style and Find Your Perfect Match.* London: Rodale, 2011.

Levine, Peter A., and Ann Frederick. *Walking the Tiger: Healing Trauma.* Berkeley, CA: North Atlantic Books, 1997.

Lionetti, Francesca, Elaine N. Aron, Arthur Aron, Daniel N. Klein, and Michael Pluess. "Observer-Rated Environmental Sensitivity Moderates Children's Response to Parenting Quality in Early Childhood." *Developmental Psychology* 55, no. 11 (2019): 2389–2402. doi.org/10.1037/dev0000795.

Neville, Morgan, dir. *Won't You Be My Neighbor?* 2018; New York: Focus Features. Film.

Orloff, Judith. *The Empath's Survival Guide. Life Strategies for Sensitive People.* Boulder, CO: Sounds True, Inc., 2018.

Perel, Esther. *Mating in Captivity: Unlocking Erotic Intelligence.* New York: Harper, 2007.

Pluess, Michael, and Jay Belsky. "Vantage Sensitivity: Individual Differences in Response to Positive Experiences." *Psychological Bulletin* 139, no. 4 (2013): 901–16 doi.org/10.1037/a0030196.

Rogers, Fred. *The World According to Mr. Rogers: Important Things to Remember.* New York: Hachette Books, 2003.

Siegel, Daniel J. *The Developing Mind: How Relationships and the Brain Interact to Shape Who We Are.* New York: The Guilford Press, 1999.

Strickland, Jacquelyn. "Introversion, Extroversion and the Highly Sensitive Person." *Psychology Today,* May 13, 2018. psychologytoday.com/us/blog /the-highly-sensitive-person/201805/introversion-extroversion-and-the -highly-sensitive-person.

Slagt, Meike, Judith Semon Dubas, Marcel A. G. Van Aken, Bruce J. Ellis, and Maja Deković. "Sensory Processing Sensitivity as a Marker of Differential Susceptibility to Parenting." *Developmental Psychology* 54, no. 3 (2018): 543–58. doi.org/10.1037/dev0000431.

Snow, April. Sensitive Therapist. Accessed April 18, 2020. sensitivetherapist .com.

Thich Nhat Hanh. *True Love: A Practice for Awakening the Heart.* Boulder, CO: Shambhala Publications, 1997.

Williams, Margery. *The Velveteen Rabbit.* London: George H. Doran Publishing, 1922.

Wolf, M., G. S. Van Doorn, and F. J. Weissing. "Evolutionary Emergence of Responsive and Unresponsive Personalities." *Proceedings of the National Academy of Sciences* 105, no. 41 (June 2008): 15825–30. doi.org/10.1073 /pnas.0805473105.

Zeff, Ted. *The Strong, Sensitive Boy: Help Your Son Become a Happy, Confident Man.* San Ramos, CA: Prana Publishing, 2010.

# INDEX

# ACKNOWLEDGMENTS

A heart-filled thank you to my mentor, Mary Myers, who has truly been a gift in my life in so many ways. Also, much appreciation to all the healers I have been honored to work with, especially the therapist of my past, Dr. Fanny Brewster, and the therapist of my present, Sharon Kleinberg, LCSW. I would not be typing these words without you both!

And a very special thank you to all my clients who have given me the gift of their experiences and have allowed me to share their stories here. I am so honored to work with all of you!

# ABOUT THE AUTHOR

**Allison Lefkowitz** is a licensed marriage and family therapist with a private practice in New York City, where she specializes in working with highly sensitive people. She lives in Sunnyside, Queens, with her husband and exceptional dog, Willis. She was born and raised in Los Angeles, California, and identifies as bicoastal.

She received her master's degree in marriage and family therapy from Hofstra University on Long Island, New York, and a bachelor's degree in theatre arts from California State University, Northridge. Allison also has a background in voiceover and improv comedy and considers all arts to be essential tools for life and healing.

Fun fact: She won the "best writer" award in her fifth-grade popularity poll.

You can contact Allison via her website, ALMFT.com, or email her at allisonlefkowitz@icloud.com.